Anatomy
of a
Business Plan

Other books and software by the same authors:

Automate Your Business Plan (see page ix)

Keeping the Books

The Home-Based Entrepreneur

Target Marketing for the Small Business

Steps to Small Business Start-Up

The Woman Entrepreneur

Anatomy
of a
Business Plan

A Step-by-Step Guide to
Starting Smart, Building the Business
and Securing Your Company's Future

Second Edition

Linda Pinson
and
Jerry Jinnett

Enterprise · Dearborn
a division of Dearborn Publishing Group, Inc.

While a great deal of care has been taken to provide accurate and current information, the ideas, suggestions, general principles and conclusions presented in this text are subject to local, state and federal laws and regulations, court cases and any revisions of same. The reader is thus urged to consult legal counsel regarding any points of law—this publication should not be used as a substitute for competent legal advice.

Publisher: Kathleen A. Welton
Production Manager: Karen Billipp
Cover and Interior Design: Phillip Augusta

© 1987, 1989 by Linda Pinson and Jerry Jinnett
Second edition Copyright © 1993 by Linda Pinson and Jerry Jinnett

Published by Enterprise • Dearborn
a division of Dearborn Publishing Group, Inc.

Printed in the United States of America

94 95 10 9 8 7 6 5 4 3

Library of Congress Cataloging-in-Publication Data

Pinson, Linda.
    Anatomy of a business plan/by Linda Pinson and Jerry Jinnett.
        p.   cm.
    Includes bibliographical references and index.
    ISBN 0-7931-0618-4
    1. Corporate planning. 2. New business enterprises—Planning.
I. Jinnett, Jerry. II. Title
HD30.28.P5   1993
658.4'012—dc20   93-18457
                                                         CIP

Dedication

It is with a great deal of pleasure that we dedicate this book to Tom Drewes, the former President of Quality Books, Inc., our mentor and friend. His kindness and encouragement were our inspiration in 1986. Because of his belief in us, our books are now being used in libraries across the nation. Thank you, Tom, for your many years of tireless dedication to independent publishers and for your willingness to share yourself with so many and ask for nothing in return.

TABLE OF CONTENTS

AUTOMATE YOUR BUSINESS PLAN 5.0

Companion Software to
"Anatomy of a Business Plan"

Technical Requirements:

- **IBM PC, AT, or 100% compatible computer**
- **No Hard Drive Needed, No Other Software Needed**
- **640K of Internal memory**
- **PCDOS/MSDOS version 2.0 or higher**
- **Any standard PC compatible printer**

THREE PROGRAMS IN ONE

1. "Automate Your Business Plan" will guide you step by step through the business planning process, calculate your spreadsheets, provide a working draft and print out a finished plan that will serve as your business guide and satisfy your lender.

2. The text editor can also be used in the stand-alone mode. It is a full-featured word processor including pull down menus and context sensitive help.

3. The spreadsheet program can also be used for other applications. You can create additional spreadsheets that might be helpful in the operation of your business. While it is not as expansive as larger programs, it is very easy to learn and should serve all your needs.

4. Text created within "Automate Your Business Plan" is standard ASCII text. That means you can readily incorporate business plans created using "Automate Your Business Plan" into documents produced by other word processors such as WordPerfect or Microsoft Word.

5. The companion book, "Anatomy of a Business Plan" is included free with the software. The authors were selected by the SBA in Washington, D.C. to write the new official business plan publication, "How to Write a Business Plan" (to be released soon), based on this book, which has been used extensively in colleges and libraries.

ORDER TODAY
(JUST FILL IN THE ORDER BLANK BELOW)

AUTOMATE YOUR BUSINESS PLAN & ANATOMY OF BUSINESS PLAN
Software & Text Pkg. @ $95.00   _____

California Residents please add 7¾% sales tax   _____

Shipping Fees $4.50

Next Day Air Express $21.00   _____

2nd Day Air Express $12.00   _____

Total Amount Due $ _____

Disk Size (check one): 3.5"_____ 5.25"_____

Prices Effective January 1994

NAME_____

ADDRESS_____

CITY _____

STATE_____ ZIP_____

TELEPHONE_____

Make Check or Money Order Payable To:

**OUT OF YOUR MIND...
AND INTO THE MARKETPLACE™**
13381 White Sand Drive
Tustin, CA 92680
Telephone: (714) 544-0248

AUTOMATE YOUR BUSINESS PLAN

NEW 5.0 VERSION

"Three Programs In One" To Insure Business Success!

PROGRAM #1 — A powerful & friendly tool for a winning business plan.

"Automate Your Business Plan, for the IBM PC takes the approach developed in the book 'Anatomy of a Business Plan' and combines it with a text editor and a spreadsheet program with predefined planning outlines, spreadsheets, templates, and instructions."

BYTE Magazine

"Automate Your Business Plan" is a straightforward and easy-to-use business plan program. All you need to do is auto-install the program and follow the simple instructions. The program will take you through all the steps to create a winning business plan that will satisfy your bankers, your investors, and you.

EASY & COMPLETE: "Automate Your Business Plan" is a powerful software program that gives you maximum flexibility with minimum confusion. The entire program operates from a series of menu-driven options designed to keep you on track and in control. You are guided through each section of the business plan with clear instructions and relevant examples. When your first draft is completed, you can go back, edit and print either individual sections or the entire business plan. This is not a throw away program. You can write, edit, and print as many business plans as your computer has room to store.

PRE-FORMULATED FINANCIAL PLANNING: You will have all the accounting tools you need to organize and present a winning plan. Financial Statements (cashflow, balance sheet, P&L, etc.) are pre-formulated. All you have to do is plug in the numbers! **"Automate Your Business Plan" gives you the results!**

PROGRAM #2 — A full-powered word processor for business communication.

Our full-featured text editor also operates outside the business plan program as a stand-alone word processor. It contains all the features you will need to create, edit, and print professional business communications. All text is created in ASCII format, which enables you to import all of your documents into your favorite word processing program such as WordPerfect® or Microsoft® Word. Pull-down menus give you easy access and control. Some additional program features include:

- ❑ Text windows to multiple documents
- ❑ Character attribute capabilities w/superscript, subscript
- ❑ Search and replace functions
- ❑ Macro features

PROGRAM #3 — A spreadsheet program to simplify financial planning.

Our spreadsheet program operates both as part of the business plan program and as a stand-alone financial tool. You can use the pre-designed, formulated financial statements. The program also contains all of the necessary tools to quickly design and run any additional accounting spreadsheets needed to run your business. Some included features in the spreadsheet program are:

- ❑ Auto calculation and recalculation features
- ❑ Easy formula creation and modification
- ❑ Automatic number formatting
- ❑ Column width adjustment
- ❑ Insert and delete rows and columns

Introduction

One of the principal reasons for business failure is the lack of an adequate plan. When we consider the concept of business planning, three critical facts always seem to surface:

1. **All businesses need a business plan.** You can fly by the seat of your pants, but you will probably get torn pants. Successful business owners are usually those who have taken the time to evaluate all the aspects of their businesses and to map their plans for the future.

2. **All lending institutions require a business plan.** Lenders and investors are sharing the risk in your business. They want to know that you are going to be successful. Your business plan is the only way they have to evaluate whether or not they should take that risk.

3. **Few business owners know how to write a business plan!** Everyone hears the terms "cash flow," "marketing plan," "fixed assets," "break-even analysis," etc. Even if a business owner understands some of these terms, it is not often that he or she has the concept of how to put them together into a workable plan. The thought of having to research and combine all of this information into a working business plan can be a heavy burden.

It is the goal of this book to take away the mystery in the business planning process. We want to give you a clear, concise, and easy-to-understand format to help you prepare a plan that will aid you either as a new business owner planning for start-up or as a currently-operating business owner who needs a vehicle for implementing changes throughout the life of your business.

Anatomy of a Business Plan was designed with the simplification of your task as its primary purpose. The first thing you should do is read the book to give you a general overview of the format and content. After reading, begin with the Organizational Plan section and complete each part before proceeding to the next topic. If any forms are needed for your work, you will find them following the text relating to that item. If you follow this step-by-step method, you will soon have a completed business plan.

An **actual business plan** is also included in this book to help you see the results that were obtained by a business owner who followed our format. You will find it in the back of the book under Appendix II. We thank Bob Garcia of "Marine Art of California" for his generosity in sharing his business plan with us and with you.

Thank you for choosing our book to help you accomplish your goal. We wish you success in writing your business plan!

—Linda Pinson & Jerry Jinnett

Business Plan Considerations

A well-written business plan can provide a pathway to profit for a new or existing business. This chapter is designed to give you some background information and guidelines to consider prior to writing your business plan.

Why do you need a business plan? If you need access to additional capital, what does the lender or investor need to know? What are the key words that make your plan more effective? These questions will be addressed in the following pages.

Purposes

What Do Investors Look For?

The "Key" To Effective Writing

Business Plan Considerations

PURPOSES

There are two main purposes for writing a business plan:

1. **THE MOST COMMON REASON** is to provide a lender with detailed information on all aspects of the company's past and current operations and to make future projections. Obviously, if you are a new business, you will not have a history. The business plan for a new company seeking funding will have to rely on the credit records and financial statements of the individuals involved in the business. These will give the lender or investor insight into the ways in which personal business is conducted. The manner in which company business is conducted often reflects one's personal management style.

2. **THE MOST IMPORTANT REASON** for writing a business plan is to develop a guide to be used throughout the lifetime of your business. The business plan is a blueprint of your business and will serve to keep you on the right track. To be of value, your plan must be kept up-to-date. While plans presented to lenders must be bound, you may choose to keep your working copy of the plan in a loose-leaf binder. Then you may add current financial statements, updated rate sheets, recent marketing information, and other data as they become available.

If you are seeking capital, the business plan details how the desired investment or loan will further the company's goals. Every banker or investor wants to know how the loan will improve the worth of your company and enable you to repay the loan (with interest) on a timely basis. You will have to detail how the money will be used and back up your figures with solid information such as estimates, industry norms, rate sheets, etc. Bankers have access to statistics that are considered normal for various industries, so be sure that your projections are reasonable.

One of the principal reasons for business failure is lack of planning. Remember:

"The business that fails to plan, plans to fail."

Take the time to write a clear, concise and winning business plan. The success of your business depends on it!

WHAT DO INVESTORS LOOK FOR?

If you are looking for lenders or investors, it is to your advantage to understand the elements that they would most want to see in a well-written business plan. Remember that bankers are people, too. Just as you will have to present your business plan to them, they will have to present your plan to their bank's loan committee. We all fear rejection. You are afraid of having your loan denied. The loan officer is fearful of presenting your plan to the committee and having it rejected. You can increase your chances of success by considering the following items. Keep them in mind as you write your plan and review them when your plan has been completed.

1. **What is your credit history?**

    Provide a credit history that demonstrates that you are a good risk. If you are an existing business, provide information about your payment history. A past bankruptcy or a history of late payments can serve as a "red flag" and send out a warning signal that you may be a bad risk. You will have to prove through a well-prepared Financial Section that you understand all of the costs involved in your business and that you have a complete understanding of cash flow. If you are a new business, your personal financial history will be examined. The banker determines your character based on your financial history.

2. **What collateral do you have?**

    What assets do you have and what are you willing to risk for the success of your business? You may be asked to use your home as collateral. You may have money in C.D.'s or other investments that will qualify. The collateral you provide shows your commitment to your company and removes some risk on the part of the bank in granting a loan.

3. **What is your repayment plan?**

    The investor wants to know that you appreciate his needs and that you have given consideration to your company's ability to repay the loan plus interest.

    a. **Any asset that you want to finance must last at least as long as the loan period.** For example, you cannot get a five-year, $25,000 loan on a piece of electronic equipment that is expected to become obsolete within two years of the date of purchase.

    b. **The asset should generate the repayment of funds.** Show in your Financial Section (specifically in your Cash Flow Projections and in your Three-Year Projected Income Statement) that the object of the loan will increase sales, increase efficiency, or cut costs and will, in turn, generate added revenue for repayment of the loan plus interest.

4. Is there a demand for your product or service?

Be prepared to show evidence that your product or service is well-received by your target market (your customers). You can demonstrate demand through a favorable sales history, accounts receivable information, or purchase orders. If you are a new service company or a business with a new product, show customer acceptance through test market results, questionnaire and survey data, and testimonials. To be valid, the responses must come from your target market and not from friends and family. Test market your product and get some evaluations. Ask people for whom you have provided your service to write testimonial letters.

5. Have you established a proprietary position?

This means that you have secured your position in the market in some manner. There is something unique about your business and you have protected this uniqueness in some way. This may be through copyright, trademark or patent. Include a copy of the document verifying such protection. If you are located in a mall or shopping center, you may be able to work with management to limit competition in some manner. For example, location of competition may be written into the terms of the lease. You may be able to ensure that you will be the only donut shop in a small shopping center or have it specified in the terms of your lease agreement that you will have no direct competition within a given radius of your store. Include a copy of your lease in the Supporting Documents section of your plan and stress any proprietary rights when you write about your location.

6. Are your projections realistic?

Base your figures on your current market share. Explain your opportunities for growth and demonstrate how you plan to make use of these opportunities. Each industry has its range of accepted financial results and market approaches. Examine the annual reports of public companies in your field. Make use of the public library or college library in your area. Read trade journals, business publications, and government and industry reports to determine trends in your business area. Work out a realistic timetable for achieving your goals. Remember that bankers judge your plan and goals in terms of your industry's practices and trends.

THE "KEY" TO EFFECTIVE WRITING

KEY WORDS

The text of the business plan must be concise and yet must contain as much information as possible. This sounds like a contradiction, but you can solve this dilemma by using the **key word** approach. Write the following key words on a card and keep it in front of you while you are writing:

WHO	**WHEN**	**UNIQUE**
WHAT	**WHY**	**BENEFIT TO THE CUSTOMER**
WHERE	**HOW**	**HOW MUCH**

Answer all of the questions asked by the key words in one paragraph at the beginning of each section of your business plan. Then expand on that thesis statement by telling more about each item in the text that follows. Stress any uniqueness and benefit to the customer which may pertain to the section in which you are writing. Examples will be given in the following chapters to give you guidance. Keep in mind that the lender's time is limited and that your plan is not the only one he or she will be reviewing. Often the first paragraph following a heading will be the only area read; therefore, it is very important to include as much pertinent and concise information as possible in that first paragraph.

EFFECTIVE USE OF YOUR TIME

There is no set length to a business plan. The average length seems to be 30 to 40 pages, including the Supporting Documents section. Break the plan down into sections. Set up blocks of time for work with target dates for completion. You may find it effective to spend two evenings per week at the library. You will not be interrupted by the telephone or tempted by the refrigerator or television set. An added bonus is that the reference material you need will be close at hand. It takes discipline, time, and privacy to write an effective business plan.

SUPPORTING DOCUMENTS

You will find it time-saving to compile your list of Supporting Documents while writing the text. For example, while writing about the legal structure of your business, you will realize the need to include a copy of your partnership agreement. Write "partnership agreement" on your list of Supporting Documents. When it comes time to compile that section of your plan, you will already have a listing of necessary documents. As you go along, request any information you do not have, such as credit reports. If you take care of gathering the necessary documents in this manner, the materials you need to complete the Supporting Documents Section will be available when you are ready to assemble it.

BUSINESS PLAN OUTLINE

With the previous considerations in mind, you are ready to begin formulating your plan. The pieces of a business plan in this book are as follows:

- **Cover Sheet**

- **Statement of Purpose**

- **The Organizational Plan**

- **The Marketing Plan**

- **Financial Documents**

- **Supporting Documents**

Each of the areas of the business planning process is covered in a separate chapter of the book. *Anatomy of a Business Plan* is designed to help you write a complete, concise and well-organized plan that will guide you and your company toward a profitable future.

The Cover Sheet

The Cover Sheet of your business plan is like the cover of a book. It needs to be attractive and should contain some important information.

The next two pages cover the following:

What to Include

Sample Cover Sheet

The Cover Sheet

WHAT TO INCLUDE

The first page of your business plan will be the cover sheet. It serves as the title page and should contain the following information:

- **Company name**
- **Company address**
- **Company phone number (including area code)**
- **Logo, if you have one**
- **Names, titles, addresses and phone numbers of the owners or corporate officers**
- **Month and year in which plan is issued**
- **Number of the copy**
- **Name of the preparer**

The company name, address, and phone number should appear in the top one-third of the page. If you have a logo, it may appear in the upper left hand corner of the page or wherever you choose.

Information regarding the owners or corporate officers of the business will appear in the center of the page.

The bottom third of the page will contain the remaining information. The month and year in which the plan was written lets the lender know if it is up-to-date. For instance, if the plan is five months old, the lender may request an update on certain financial information. Some lenders prefer that the plan be written by one or more of the business owners or officers. This signifies a hands-on approach to the running of the company. Numbering your copies helps you keep track of them. Keep a log with the following information: number of copy, name of person reviewing the copy, reviewer's phone number and date submitted. This way you can keep up with the reviewing process and can make follow-up calls to the lender if necessary.

THE COVER SHEET ■ 9

A sample cover sheet follows for your use. As you can see, this one page contains a good amount of information. It provides the name, location, and phone number of your business. By listing the sole proprietor, partners, or corporate officers, the lender knows the legal structure of the business and knows how to contact key people directly for additional information. Keep in mind that lenders must review many business plans in a limited amount of time. It is to your advantage to aid the lender by making your plan thorough and concise.

Sample Cover Sheet

ABC CORPORATION
372 East Main Street
Burke, NY 10071
(207) 526-4319

John Smith, President
742 South Street
Jamestown, NY 10081
(207) 814-0221

Mary Blake, Vice-President
86 West Avenue
Burke, NY 10071
(207) 764-1213

James Lysander, Secretary
423 Potrero Avenue
Jessup, NY 10602
(207) 842-1648

Tandi Higgins, Treasurer
321 Nason Street
Adams, NY 10604
(207) 816-0201

Plan prepared August, 1993
by the Corporate Officers

Copy 2 of 6

Statement of Purpose

The Statement of Purpose is the thesis statement of your business plan. Although it appears near the front of the plan, it is most effectively written after the rest of your business plan is completed. At that time, all the information and financial data needed will be available.

Use the **Key Word** approach mentioned earlier in the book. In a concise, one-page statement you will sum up the essence of your business plan by including answers to the following questions:

What?

Where?

When?

Why?

How?

Statement of Purpose

STATEMENT OF PURPOSE

The Statement of Purpose is the thesis statement of your business plan. You may also hear it referred to as the "mission statement" or "summary statement." If the lender were to read only the statement of purpose, he would know the name and nature of your business, its legal structure, the amount and purpose of your loan request, and a repayment statement. If your business plan is for internal use only and you are not seeking funds, this statement would be a summary of your business and its goals for the future.

Use the **key word** approach mentioned earlier in this book. Be concise and clear. The statement of purpose is contained on one page. As you write your business plan and refine your ideas, you will probably discover new ideas and information that you will want to incorporate into your business plan to make your business more effective and profitable. For this reason, the statement of purpose is most effectively written after your plan has been completed. At that time, all the information and financial data will be available and you can draw it from the written text and financial spreadsheets.

The following is an example of how the key words may be used to help you form your Statement of Purpose:

What

What is the business name?
(ABC Corporation)

What is its legal structure?
(S Corporation)

What product or service is involved?
(Manufacturer of specialized parts for the aerospace industry)

What will the loan do for the company?
(Modernize equipment, which will result in a 35% increase in production and decrease the unit cost by 25%)

What will be used for collateral?
(Property at 372 E. Main Street, Burke, NY, with an assessed valuation of $185,000 in 1992)

Where

Where is the business located?
(372 E. Main Street, Burke, NY 10071)

Why

Why is the loan needed?
(To increase growth capital)

How

How much money is needed?
($100,000)

How will the loan be used?
(For the purchase of new and more modern equipment and to train personnel in the use of the new equipment)

How will the loan be repaid?
(The end result will be a net profit increase sufficient to repay the loan and interest within 3 years)

When

When was the business established?
(1987)

When is the loan needed?
(Funding is needed so equipment can be delivered and in place by January 11, 1994. There is a two-month period between order placement and delivery date.)

When can repayment begin?
(Within 30 days of receipt of funds)

If you are writing your plan for a lender, be specific about the use of funds. Support the amount requested with information such as purchase orders, estimates from suppliers, rate sheets and marketing results. Include this information in the Supporting Documents section. For example, if you are purchasing a piece of equipment in order to increase production or expand services, you must not only show figures on its cost, but must also demonstrate a ready market for the additional products or services. The rest of the plan must back up your summary statement.

Address the question of loan repayment. You want to show the lender your company's ability to meet interest expense as well as principal. Some investors like to see "two ways out"—two different sources of repayment.

When you have answered the key word questions, you are ready to present that information in one or two concise paragraphs.

Note: A sample statement of purpose using the key word information in this section follows to serve as a guide.

Sample of a Statement of Purpose

Statement of Purpose

for

ABC CORPORATION

ABC Corporation, an S Corporation established in 1987, is a tool and die company that manufactures specialized parts for the aerospace industry and is located at 372 E. Main Street, Burke, NY. The company is seeking growth capital in the amount of $100,000 for the purpose of purchasing new and more modern equipment and for training existing personnel in the use of that new equipment.

Funding is needed in time for the equipment to be delivered and in place by January 11, 1994. There is a two-month period between order placement and delivery date.

The modernized equipment will result in a 35% increase in production and will decrease the unit cost by 25%. Repayment of the loan and interest can begin promptly within 30 days of receipt of funds. The loan can be further secured by company-owned real estate that has a 1992 assessed valuation of $185,000.

Part I:
The Organizational Plan

The first major section of your business plan covers the organizational details of your business. Include information about your industry in general and your business in particular.

Again using the key words, address all of the following elements. There is no set format for their arrangement. You may cover each item in an order that seems logical to you.

Description of the Business

Legal Structure

Products or Services

Location

Management

Personnel

Methods of Recordkeeping

Insurance

Security

The Organizational Plan

Begin this section with a one-page summary addressing the key elements of your business. The lender should have a clear picture of the origins and objectives of your company. Indicate where the company is going and how it is going to get there. The text following your business summary will expand on each area presented. Be prepared to back up statements and justify projections with data in the Supporting Documents section.

You may formulate the organizational plan by again using the **key word** system. Answer the questions as they relate to each of the areas to be addressed in this section. There is no set format for their arrangement. Cover each topic in an order that seems logical to you. Remember, you are writing a **summary**. Be concise.

DESCRIPTION OF THE BUSINESS

This is the section of the plan in which you present a brief summary of the organization of your business, its business history, its present status, and your future projections for research and development. Stress the uniqueness of your product or service and state how you can benefit the customer. Project a sense of what you expect to accomplish three to five years into the future.

Answer such questions as when and why this company was formed, the nature of the services or products provided, how the company developed and what is being projected for the future.

Example: The following is a sample Description of Business statement for ABC Corporation:

> ABC Corporation was established in 1987 to meet the demand for specialized parts for the aerospace industry. This industry experienced moderate growth with an increase in contracts beginning in 1992. Industry projections indicate a growing demand for the type of products the company manufactures. ABC Corporation maintains a competitive edge with prompt order fulfillment, excellent customer relations, and custom design capabilities. The company is adequately housed in a 25,000 square foot facility and desires to meet the growing demand for its products through the purchase of new and more modern equipment, which will provide the opportunity for broader scope bidding, increased custom design capabilities, lower per unit costs and faster turnaround time.

After completing the "Description of Business" statement, expand on each of the following topics:

LEGAL STRUCTURE

State the reasons for your choice of legal structure. If you are a sole proprietor, you may include a copy of your business license in the Supporting Documents section.

If you have formed a partnership, include a copy of your partnership agreement in the Supporting Documents section. Your agreement should include provisions for partners to exit and for the dissolution of the company. It must spell out the distribution of the profits and the financial responsibility for any losses. Explain the reasoning behind the terms of the agreement.

If you have formed a corporation, explain why this legal form was chosen and how the company will operate within the corporate structure. Include a copy of the charter and articles in the Supporting Documents section.

If you anticipate changing your legal structure in the future, make projections regarding why you would change, when the change would take place, who would be involved, and how the change would benefit the company. Refer back to this section for information on legal structure when completing the Business Financial Statement or Loan Application form from a lender.

PRODUCTS OR SERVICES

If You Are Involved in the
Manufacture and Distribution of a Product

Give a detailed description of the development of that product from raw materials to finished item. Develop a flow chart. It will help you identify stages of production and will serve as a visual representation of product development for the lender.

What raw materials are used and how much do they cost? Project peak production times and determine when money will be needed for key purchases. This financial information will be transferred to the Cash Flow Statement in your Financial Documents section. Write about the value and amount of inventory you plan to keep. Who will be taking inventory and when will this occur? Inventory information will later be transferred to the Loan Application form provided by a lender.

Who are your suppliers, where are they located and why did you choose them? Include cost breakdowns and rate sheets in the Supporting Documents section to back up your statements. Although you may order from one main supplier, include information on alternate suppliers. Address how you could handle a sudden increase of orders or a loss of a major supplier. How will the work get done, by whom and at what cost? You will use labor cost projections again when you develop a Cash Flow Statement in your Financial Documents section.

Describe your equipment and facilities. Information on vehicles, equipment and buildings owned by your company will appear as Balance Sheet items in the Financial Documents section of your plan. When preparing your Balance Sheet, you will refer to this section for information on current values.

You may hear a lender refer to **the worst-case scenario**. This means that the lender wants you to be able to anticipate and solve potential problems. It is also to your advantage to think in terms of alternatives and to prepare for the unexpected so that your business can continue to run smoothly. Some businesses fail because they become too successful too soon. Therefore, it is also good to plan for **the best-case scenario**. If you are inundated with orders, your business plan should contain the information needed to hire staff and contact additional suppliers. Your business plan is your key to responding promptly to the unexpected in order to keep your business progressing smoothly.

If You Are Providing a Service

Tell what your service is, why you are able to provide it, how it is provided, who will be doing the work and where the service will be performed. Tell why your business is unique and what you have that is special to offer to your customers. If you have both a product and a service that work together to benefit your customer (such as warranty service for the products you sell), be sure to mention this in your plan. State where you will be getting your supplies and why those suppliers were chosen. Project the costs of overhead and vehicle expense. Will you be providing service in the customer's home or will you work from an office? How much time is involved in the service you will be doing and how many of those hours are billable to the client?

In all Cases

List future services or products that you plan to add to your business. Try to anticipate potential problem areas and work out a plan of action. You should state any proprietary rights, such as copyright, patent or trademark in this section. You will need to back up your statements by including copies of photos, diagrams and certificates in the Supporting Documents section.

LOCATION

If location is a marketing consideration, it will not be included in this section. For example, if you are opening a retail shop and need to be directly accessible to your customers, your choice of location will be determined by your target market and would therefore need to be addressed in your Marketing Plan (see Chapter 5). If you are a manufacturer, however, and ship by common carrier such as United Parcel Service, your location may not be directly tied to your target market. In that case, you would discuss location **here** in your Organizational Plan. You may begin with a sentence such as:

> **ABC Corporation is housed in 25,000 square feet of warehouse space located at 372 E. Main Street, Burke, NY. This space was chosen because of accessibility to shipping facilities, good security provisions, low square footage costs, and proximity to sources of supply.**

Now expand on each reason and back up your statements with a physical description of the site and a copy of the lease agreement. Your lease or rental agreement will contain the financial information needed for monthly cost projections for the Cash Flow statement. The value of property owned will be transferred to a Balance Sheet in the Financial Documents section.

Give background information on your site choice. List other possible locations and tell why you chose your location. You may want to include copies of pictures, layouts or drawings of the location in the Supporting Documents section.

A **Location Analysis Worksheet** is included at the end of this section. You may duplicate it for your own use in gathering data needed to make a decision regarding the location of your business. This worksheet is intended as a guideline for writing a location (site) analysis. Cover only those topics that are relevant to your business.

MANAGEMENT

This section describes who is behind the business. If you are a sole proprietor, tell about your abilities and include your resume. Also be honest about areas in which you will need help and state how you will get that help. Will you take a marketing seminar, work with an accountant or seek the advice of someone in advertising?

If you have formed a partnership, explain why the partners were chosen, what they bring to the company and how their abilities complement each other. Experience, background and qualifications will be covered in their resumes, which will be included in the Supporting Documents section. If you have incorporated, outline the corporate structure and give detailed information on the corporate officers. Who are they, what are their skills, why were they chosen and what will they bring to the organization?

PERSONNEL

Who will be doing the work, why are they qualified, how will they be hired, what is their wage, what will they be doing? Outline their duties and include job descriptions. Include copies of any employee contracts. Explain any employee benefits. If you are inundated with orders for your product or items to be serviced, do you have a plan for increasing personnel? For example, if you project a volume of business that would warrant hiring additional staff in 6 months, project the additional salaries and transfer those amounts to the Cash Flow Statement.

METHODS OF RECORDKEEPING

Tell what accounting system will be used and why the system was chosen. What portion of your record keeping will be done internally? Who will be responsible for keeping those records? Will you be using an outside accountant to maximize your profits? If so, who within your company will be skilled at reading and analyzing the financial statements provided by the accountant? It is important to show not only that your accounting will be taken care of, but that you will have some means of using your financial statements to implement changes to make your company more profitable. After reading this section, the lender should have confidence in your company's ability to keep and interpret a complete set of financial records. Information regarding recordkeeping and auditing of your books is often requested on the Business Financial Statement from the lender.

INSURANCE

Insurance is an important consideration for every business. Product liability is a major consideration, especially in certain industries. Service businesses are concerned with personal liability, insuring customers' goods while on the premises or during the transporting of those goods. If a vehicle is used for business purposes, your insurance must reflect that use. If you own your business location, you will need property insurance. Some types of businesses require bonding. Partners may want life insurance naming each other as the beneficiary. Consider the types of coverage appropriate to your business. Tell what coverage you have, why you chose it, what time period it covers and who the carrier is.

Keep your insurance information current. An **Insurance Update Form** has been included at the end of this section. Use it to maintain information on alternate insurance companies. If your premiums are suddenly raised, you will be able to refer to your worksheet in order to find another insurance carrier. The Business Financial Statement from the lender asks for information that can be taken from this section.

SECURITY

According to the U.S. Chamber of Commerce, more than 30% of business failures result from employee dishonesty. This includes not only theft of merchandise, but also theft of information.

Address the issue of security as it relates to your business. For example, if you are disposing of computer printout data, a small paper shredder may be cost-effective. We have all seen the sensing devices used in clothing stores. Anticipate problem areas in your business, identify security measures you will put into practice and tell why you chose them, and what you project they will accomplish. Discuss this area with your insurance agent. You may be able to lower certain insurance costs while protecting your business.

SUMMARY

You have now covered all the areas that should be addressed in the Organizational Plan. Use the key words, be thorough, anticipate any problem areas and be prepared with solutions, analyze industry trends and be ready to project your business into the future. Chapter 11, "Information Resources" contains listings of resource materials available to you. Most are available at your public or college library. Use them to gather the information needed to write a comprehensive business plan. When the Organization Plan section has been completed, you are ready to go to the next chapter and begin formulating the Marketing Plan.

Location Analysis Worksheet

1. Address:

2. Name, address, phone number of realtor/contact person:

3. Square footage/cost:

4. History of location:

5. Location in relation to your target market:

6. Traffic patterns for customers:

7. Traffic patterns for suppliers:

8. Availability of parking (include diagram):

9. Crime rate for the area:

10. Quality of public services (e.g., police, fire protection):

11. Notes on walking tour of the area:

12. Neighboring shops and local business climate:

13. Zoning regulations:

14. Adequacy of utilities (get information from utility company representatives):

15. Availability of raw materials/supplies:

16. Availability of labor force:

17. Labor rate of pay for the area:

18. Housing availability for employees:

19. Tax rates (state, county, income, payroll, special assessments):

20. Evaluation of site in relation to competition:

INSURANCE UPDATE FORM

COMPANY	CONTACT PERSON	COVERAGE	COST

CHAPTER

V

Part II:
The Marketing Plan

The second major section of your business plan covers the details of your marketing plan. In this section you will include information about the total market with an emphasis on your own target market.

Again using the key words, address all of the following elements. There is no set format for their arrangement. Cover each item in an order that seems logical to you.

Target Market

Competition

Methods of Distribution

Promotion

Pricing

Product Design

Timing of Market Entry

Location

Industry Trends

The Marketing Plan

WHAT IS A MARKETING PLAN?

Your Marketing Plan is the section of your business plan that is devoted to getting your product or service to your customer or "target market." You might like to think of marketing as the **Three Rs Process**. You will need to (1) **research**, (2) **reach** and (3) **retain** your target market. The elements included in this chapter should help you to organize needed information into a workable plan that will do just that.

A good marketing plan is essential to your business development and success. It will be necessary for you to include information about the total market with emphasis on your target market. You must take the time to identify your customers and find the means to make your product or service attractive and available to them. The key here is **time**. It takes time to re-search and develop a good marketing plan, but it is time well spent.

Most of the information you need will be found in the public library and in the publications of the U.S. Department of Commerce, the U.S. Small Business Administration (SBA), and the U.S. Census Bureau (see Chapter 11, "Information Resources" for specific resources). Remember, you need a clear understanding of who will purchase your product, who will make use of your service, why they will choose your company and how they will find out about it.

Begin this section with a one-page summary covering the key elements of your marketing plan. The text following will expand on each area presented in the summary. Back up statements and justify projections with data in the Supporting Documents section. Again, the key word approach will help you to thoroughly cover each area. The topics may be covered in any order that seems logical to you.

TARGET MARKET

The target market has been defined as "that group of customers with a set of common characteristics that distinguishes them from other customers." You want to identify that "set of common characteristics" that will make those customers yours.

Tell how you did your market research. What were your resources and what were your results? What are the demographics of your target market? Where do your customers live, work and shop? Do they shop where they live or where they work? What is their psychological make-up? Are they impulse purchasers? If you are in the business of VCR repair, how many VCRs are owned within a specific radius of your shop? Would in-home service be cost-effective and a benefit to your customers? What are their demographics in terms of age, sex and income? What do they do in their leisure time? Back up your findings with census reports, questionnaires, test marketing results. State how you feel you can serve this market in terms of your resources, strengths and weaknesses. Focus on reasonable, believable and obtainable projections regarding the size of your potential market.

Note: A **Target Market Worksheet** has been included at the end of this chapter for your use in identifying your customers. Complete the questions asked on the worksheet in outline format. Then formulate the information gathered into text. After reading this section, the lender must know that you have identified your customers and that you have data to support your findings.

COMPETITION

Direct competition is a business offering the same product or service to the same market. **Indirect competition** is a company with the same product or service but with a different target market. For example, a gift shop is in direct competition with another gift shop and in indirect competition with a catalog company that offers the same products. If you are a CPA who goes to the client, your indirect competition will be CPAs working in an office. The difference between direct and indirect competition is most often determined by the method of delivering your product or service.

Evaluate both types of competitors. You want to determine the competitors' images. To what part of the market are they trying to appeal? Can you appeal to the same market in a better way? Or can you find an untapped market?

Use the **Competition Evaluation Worksheet** at the end of this section to compile, organize and evaluate information about your competition. Your analysis of this information will help you plan your market entry. What is the competition's current market share (what percent of the total customer base is theirs)? Can you tap into this share or will you need to carve out your own market niche (your wedge of the pie)? Make a comparison of your competitor's pricing structure and product or service quality.

To help you with your research, we have also provided a **"Competition Reference List for Locating Information on Companies."**

After completing a competition analysis, you and your lender will know who your competitors are, where they are located, what products or services they offer, how you plan to compete, how your customers can access your business, and why you can provide a unique and beneficial service or product.

METHODS OF DISTRIBUTION

Distribution is the manner in which products are physically transported to the consumer and the way services are made available to the customer. Distribution is closely related to your target market.

Establish the purchasing patterns of your customers. If you are selling a product, do your customers purchase by direct mail, buy through catalogs, or make in-store purchases? Will you sell directly through a manufacturer's representative? If you are shipping the product, who will absorb the shipping costs and what carrier will be used?

Use the **key words** to answer questions regarding your distribution plan. Back up decisions with statistical reports, rate sheets for shippers, contracts with manufacturer's reps or any other supporting documents.

If you are involved in a service business, will you provide in-shop service? Will you make house calls, and if so, how will mileage costs be handled? What is your planned response time to fill your customers' needs?

List the pros and cons of the various methods of distribution and give the reasons for your choices. Keep in mind the **worst-case scenarios** mentioned in the business section. Present alternatives. For example, if your mobile service van breaks down, do you have a vehicle that could be used as back-up? If you are the only service provider, how will you keep your customer happy if you are ill or away from your business for a period of time? Provide for a smooth business flow. Project costs for one year and break them down into monthly expenditures. These amounts will be transferred to a Cash Flow Statement.

PROMOTION

Promotion of your business involves using all means available to get the message to your customers that your product or service is good and desirable.

You will have identified what is **unique** about your business and how that uniqueness will **benefit the customer.** The uniqueness and benefits of your products or services will carry through all of your promotion and will develop your image. The following paragraphs discuss some types of promotion to be considered while you are writing your plan:

A.   **PAID ADVERTISING** is one means of promotion and is available through radio, television, newspapers and magazines. To be effective, your promotion must be tailored for your target market. What magazines and newspapers do they read? Analyze your competitors' advertising in these publications. Your marketing research will have spelled out which television programs, radio stations and publications are of interest to your target market. In the example of ABC Corporation, trade publications and the business section of your key newspapers would be appropriate. Be ready to back up your decisions. Tell the lender where you will put your advertising dollars, why you chose those methods, how your message will reach your customers, when your advertising campaign will begin, how much your plan will cost and what format your advertising will take. Include copies of your advertisements and rate sheets in the Supporting Documents section.

B.   **DIRECTORY LISTINGS** such as the telephone Yellow Pages or trade and professional directories are another means of promoting your business. Be aware that directories are published at various times of the year. What is their publication schedule, what costs will be incurred for the listing, what are the circulation figures, what segment of your target market has access to these directories and how will this be cost effective? Costs will be transferred to your Cash Flow Statement.

C.   **PUBLICITY** is "**free**" media coverage you have received or plan to seek. Include samples of press releases you will send and a plan for contacting key media people. You will find listings of media in the reference section of your library. Include copies of media coverage you have received in the Supporting Documents section. Explain who you plan to contact, when you plan to contact them, what promotional angle you will present, and how you plan to capitalize on that publicity. Publicity can be very valuable to your business and can greatly enhance your credibility. When you pay for an advertisement, you are telling the customer that your product or service is good. When a member of the media or someone else outside of your organization gives your product or service a boost, it is perceived as impartial judgment and may be worth several paid advertisements.

D. **DIRECT MAIL** can be an effective way to deliver specific information to large numbers of people. Direct mail can take the form of inexpensive fact sheets, letters, promotional gimmicks, contests, discount coupons and brochures. Tell how you will choose your mailing list, what will be sent and what response you expect. If you have already used direct mail, detail the results. How large was the mailing? How many responses were received? Was it cost-effective? Would you use direct mail in the future? Include samples of all promotional pieces in the Supporting Documents section.

E. **BUSINESS AND COMMUNITY INVOLVEMENT** through participation in trade shows and community events and membership in civic and business organizations is another means of promotion. Membership dues, subscriptions to trade publications and fees for conference attendance and participation are all costs that should be projected and included on the Cash Flow Statement.

In Summary: Tell the lender where you plan to put your promotional dollars, why you have chosen those avenues, how your message will reach your target market, when your promotional campaign will begin, how much your plan will cost and what format your advertising will take. Your timing of market entry or when you will actually start your business or introduce a new product or service may be tied to your promotional schedule. For example, if you plan to start your business during the holiday season and the new phone directories are published in November, you may be required to place your ad in July for inclusion. Since ABC Corporation plans to increase production by 35% beginning in January of 1994, the company will have to commit to certain advertising and promotion in the previous year in order to be timely and effective in creating additional buyers. Contact your promotional resources to determine their publication schedules.

PRICING

Your pricing structure is critical to the success of your business and is determined through market research and analysis of financial considerations. Basic marketing strategy is to price within the range between the **price ceiling** and the **price floor**. The price ceiling is determined by the market. It is the highest cost a consumer will pay for a product or service and is based on perceived value. What is the competition charging? What is the quality of the product or service you are offering? What is the nature of the demand and what is the image you are projecting? The price floor is the lowest amount at which you can offer a product or service, meet all of your costs and still make your desired profit. Consider all costs: manufacturing costs, variable expenses, office overhead, interest expenses and tax expense. The price floor will also have to take into account your desired annual profit. In addition to paying your costs, the revenues of the business must generate a profit. The viable business operates between the price ceiling and price floor. The difference allows for discounts, bad debt, and returns. Justify your pricing schedule based on the above considerations. Be specific as to how you arrived at your pricing structure and leave room for some flexibility.

Positioning or predetermining the perceived value in the eyes of the consumer can be accomplished through promotional activities. To be successful, you must decide what your product or service offers that your competitor's does not and promote it as the unique benefit. Very few items on the market have universal appeal—your product or service cannot be all things to all people. However, if you focus and position your product or service properly, prospective purchasers or users will immediately recognize its benefits to them. A "market mix" involving complementary products or total package services can benefit the customer and may enable you to charge an acceptably higher price.

PRODUCT DESIGN

Packaging and product design can play a major role in the success of your business. It's what first catches the customer's eye. Consider the tastes of your target market in the ultimate design of your product and your package. Decide what will be most appealing in terms of size, shape, color, material, and wording. Packaging attracts a great deal of public attention. Be advised of the Fair Packaging and Labeling Act which established mandatory labeling requirements. The Food and Drug Administration has strict procedures for labeling of items falling within its jurisdiction. The packaging guidelines can be obtained by contacting the agency or referring to a copy of the regulations in the library.

Follow the same format of using key words to answer questions regarding your product design and packaging. Include sketches or photos. Also include information on any proprietary rights such as copyright, trademark, or patent. Be sure to interpret your plans in terms of financial requirements and use that information to help you determine projections on cost of goods to be sold.

TIMING OF MARKET ENTRY

The timing of your entry into the marketplace is critical and takes careful planning and research. Having your products and services available at the right time and the right place is more a matter of understanding "consumer readiness" than your organizational schedule. The manner in which a new product is received by the consumer can be affected by the seasons, the weather and the holidays.

Early January and September are the best times to mail fliers and catalogs as consumers seem to be more receptive to mail order purchasing in those months. The major gift shows are held in the summer months (June, July, August) and again in January and February. Most wholesale buying takes place at these shows. November and December are not good months for introducing most new service businesses unless they relate in some way to the holiday season. Spring is a better time to introduce a service. There may also be other considerations that come into play. For example, if your main avenue of advertising is the Yellow Pages and it comes out in November, you will need to plan your market entry accordingly.

Information from your trade journals and trade associations will help you determine the timing patterns for your industry. Tell when you plan to enter the market and how you arrived at your decision.

LOCATION

If your choice of location is related to your target market, you will cover it in this section. For example, the location of a retail store is a marketing decision. It must be located near its target market or customers, provide adequate parking and satisfy zoning regulations.

List the reasons for your choice of location. What is the character of the neighborhood? Does the site project your business image? Where is the competition in the area? What are the traffic patterns? What are the terms of the lease? What services, if any, does the landlord provide? What is the occupancy history of your location? Did any companies in the area go out of business within the past few months? If so, try to find out if it was related to location? Is the area in which you plan to locate supported by a strong economic base? What alternate sites were considered? The chambers of commerce, police departments and city planning commissions may be able to supply you with information that will help you to determine the best location.

Note: Use the **"Location Analysis Worksheet"** provided at at the end of the Organizational Plan section. You may also refer to **Location** in Chapter 4 for additional information.

INDUSTRY TRENDS

Be alert to changes in your industry. The wise business owner follows industry trends, analyzes the economy, projects "best and worst case scenarios" and looks for ways to keep the business healthy.

Trade and professional associations and their journals and industry reports for your field will help you to write about this area. New technology may bring new products into the marketplace which will generate new service businesses. Project how your market may change and what you plan to do to keep up. For example, **"The Gift Reporter,"** a trade journal for gift retailers, indicated in 1986 that there was an interest in products featuring dinosaurs. We now see stuffed dinosaurs, dinosaurs on coffee mugs, dinosaur cereal and dinosaur motif clothing. Trends can carry over to many other industries. What is being projected for your industry? What new products or services are being developed? How do you plan to keep up with this development? **"U.S. Industrial Outlook"** is a reference which profiles many industries and gives projections for future trends. Other references are listed in Chapter 11, "Information Resources."

Analyze the economy and be aware of financial and political forecasts. For example, ABC Corporation manufactures specialized parts for the aerospace industry. Will there be a continued demand for such parts? If there are cutbacks in the federal budget, could ABC retool and go after new contracts? Read government reports and business magazines and newspapers.

Project some best- and worst-case scenarios for the future. Do some analysis regarding how much time and money would be spent in changing the focus of your business in order to remain competitive. These considerations can be translated into financial projections in order to determine if the business can remain viable.

Answer questions such as: How can the business remain competitive? What is the best case scenario for the business? What are some of the worst-case scenarios? What costs will be incurred in order to keep growing my business?" Include copies of industry reports in the Supporting Documents section as back-up for your decisions.

WORKSHEETS AND REFERENCES

The following pages contain the worksheets mentioned in this chapter. Use the Reference Section of this book to obtain sources that will help you gather information for answering your key word questions. When you have covered all of the areas addressed in the Marketing Plan, you will be ready to begin work on the Financial Documents section.

Target Market Worksheet

1. WHO ARE MY CUSTOMERS?

    a. Economic level (Income range):

    b. Sex:

    c. Age range:

    d. Psychological make-up (Lifestyle):

    e. Buying habits:

2. LOCATION

    a. Where do my customers live?

    b. Where do they work?

    c. Where do they shop?

3. PROJECTED SIZE OF MARKET:

4. WHAT ARE THE CUSTOMERS' NEEDS?

a.

b.

c.

d.

f.

5. HOW CAN I MEET THOSE NEEDS?

a.

b.

c.

d.

f.

6. WHAT IS UNIQUE ABOUT MY BUSINESS?

Complete the questions asked on the worksheet in outline format. Then formulate the information gathered into text.

Competition Reference List
(for locating information on companies)

Is the company publicly owned or privately owned/closely held?
1. *Directory of Companies Required to File Annual Reports with the SEC.*

Does the company have a parent company or subsidiaries?
1. *Directory of Corporate Affiliations.*
2. *International Directory of Corporate Affiliations.*
3. *America's Corporate Families.*

Do you need to know the company's type of business, executive officers, number of employees, annual sales?
1. *Standard & Poor's Register of Corporations.*
2. *Dun and Bradstreet's Million Dollar Directory.*
3. *Ward's Business Directory of Largest U.S. Companies.*
4. *Career Guide: Dun's Employment Opportunities Directory.*
5. *Standard Directory of Advertisers.*

Do you need the company's corporate background and financial data?
1. *Standard & Poor's Corporate Records.*
2. *Moody's Manuals.*
3. *Walker's Manual of Western Corporations.*

Is the company newsworthy?
1. *Predicasts F & S Index.*
2. *Business Periodicals Index.*

Is the company listed in a specialized directory?
1. *Thomas Register of American Manufacturers.*
2. *Best's Insurance Reports.*
3. *Standard Directory of Advertising Agencies.*
4. *U.S.A. Oil Industry Directory.*
5. *Who's Who in Electronics.*
6. *Fairchild's Financial Manual of Retail Stores.*
7. *World Aviation Directory.*
8. *Medical and Healthcare Marketplace Guide.*

How does the company rank in the industry?
1. Annual issues of *Fortune, Forbes, Inc.* and *Business Week.*
2. *Dun's Business Rankings.*

Note: Contact the reference librarian in the business section of your community or college library for availability and use of these references. Many libraries have computer services and data bases available.

Competition Evaluation Worksheet

1.   **COMPETITOR:**

2.   **LOCATION:**

3.   **PRODUCTS OR SERVICES OFFERED:**

4.   **METHODS OF DISTRIBUTION:**

5.   **IMAGE:**

    a. **Packaging:**

    b. **Promotional materials:**

    c. **Methods of advertising:**

    d. **Quality of product or service:**

6.   **PRICING STRUCTURE:**

7.   **BUSINESS HISTORY & CURRENT PERFORMANCE:**

8.   **MARKET SHARE** (number, types and location of customers):

9.   **STRENGTHS** (the strengths of the competition can become your strengths):

10.   **WEAKNESSES** (looking at the weaknesses of the competition can help you find ways of being unique and of benefiting the customer):

Note: A Competition Evaluation Worksheet should be made for each competitor. Keep these records and update them. It pays to continue to rate your competition throughout the lifetime of your business.

CHAPTER
VI

Part III:
Financial Documents

As was stipulated earlier, the body of a Business Plan is divided into three main sections. Having dealt with the first two, the Organizational and Marketing Plans, you are now ready to develop the third area of your plan.

Financial Documents are those records used to show past, current and projected finances. In this section we will cover the following which are the major documents you will want to consider and include in your Business Plan. They will consist of both pro forma (projected) and actual financial statements. Your work will be easier if these are done in the order presented.

Summary of Financial Needs

Loan Fund Dispersal Statement

Cash Flow Statement (Budget)

Three-Year Income Projection

Break-Even Analysis

Balance Sheet

Profit & Loss Statement

Loan Application/Financial History

Financial Documents

Warning on the Order of Preparation

You are now beginning the Financial Document section of your business plan. We would strongly suggest that you prepare these documents in the order that we have presented them because it will simplify the process. In the same way that a house builder must lay the foundation, build the walls and finally put on the roof, you will find that your financial statements will build on each other. Each one will use information from the ones previously done. If you try to jump ahead, you will make your task more difficult.

PURPOSE OF FINANCIAL DOCUMENTS

In the first two sections, you have written about the physical setup of your operation and your plans for finding and reaching your customers. The Financial Documents will now enable you to interpret all of that information into actual financial figures and to look realistically at your business in terms of profitability. It is often the first section turned to by a potential lender or investor.

The financial documents included in your plan are not just for the purpose of satisfying a potential lender or investor. As stated earlier, the primary reason for writing a business plan is so that it will serve as a guide during the lifetime of your business. It is extremely important that you keep updating frequently. This means examining your financials on a periodic basis, measuring your actual performance against your projections and revising your new projections accordingly.

TYPES OF FINANCIAL DOCUMENTS

There are three types of financial documents covered in this section. Before you begin your work, it is best to understand what they are and the purpose of each.

1. **Statements of Your Needs and Uses of Funds from a lender or investor.** The first two documents covered are the "Summary of Financial Needs" and the "Loan Fund Dispersal Statement." These two documents are the only ones that are written in paragraph form rather than as spreadsheets in rows and columns. They are included only if your business is seeking funds from a lender or investor (or other source).

2. **Pro Forma Statements** - The word "pro forma" in accounting means "projected." These are the statements that are used for you to predict the future profitability of your business. You are not magic and will not be able to be 100% right. However, your projections should be based on realistic research and reasonable assumptions. It is dangerous to overstate your revenues and understate your expenses.

3. **Actual Performance Statements** - These are the historical financial statements reflecting the past performance of your business. If you are planning a new business, you have no history. Therefore, you will not have these statements to include. However, once you have been in business for even one accounting period, you will have a Profit & Loss Statement and a Balance Sheet for those periods.

HOW TO PROCEED

The financial documents will be presented in the order discussed in the paragraphs above. It will be necessary for you to determine your individual situation and decide which documents to include. Below are five descriptions. Decide which one fits your business and proceed accordingly.

1. **If yours is a new business and you are going to seek a lender or investor:**

   Include the "Application of Loan Funds" and the "Loan Fund Dispersal Statement." You will also include all of the pro forma statements. You have no financial history and cannot include actual performance statements.

2. **If yours is a new business and you are not going to seek a lender or investor:**

   You will not include the "Application of Loan Funds" and the "Loan Fund Dispersal Statement." You will include all pro forma statements.

3. **If yours is an existing business and you are going to seek a lender or investor:**

   You will need to include all financial documents discussed in this chapter.

4. **If yours is an existing business and you are not seeking a lender or investor:**

   You will include all financial documents discussed in this chapter with the exception of the "Application of Loan Funds" and the "Loan Fund Dispersal Statement."

5. **If this business plan is being written for a division within a larger business:**

   Consider your division as being a business within a business and include as indicated in 1-4.

Now you are ready to prepare your financial documents. The three types will be presented in the following order:

1. Statements of financial needs and uses of funds from a lender or investor

2. Pro forma statements

3. Actual financial statements

Statements of Financial Needs
and
Uses of Funds from a Lender or Investor

The two documents covered on the following pages describe your needs for capital to be infused into your company through borrowed or invested funds. They also outline your intended use of those funds.

Include the two following statements only if you are seeking funds from a lender or investor.

The two documents are:

Summary of Financial Needs

Loan Fund Dispersal Statement

SUMMARY OF FINANCIAL NEEDS

If you are applying for a loan, your lenders and investors will analyze the requirements of your business. They will distinguish among the three types of capital as follows:

Working capital: fluctuating needs to be repaid through cash (liquidity) during the business's next full operating cycle, generally one year.

Growth capital: needs to be repaid with profits over a period of a few years. If you seek growth capital, you will be expected to show how the capital will be used to increase your business profits enough to be able to repay the loan (plus interest) within several years (usually not more than seven).

Equity capital: permanent needs. If you seek equity capital, it must be raised from investors who will take the risk for dividend returns or capital gains, or a specific share of the business.

Keeping the above in mind, you must now prepare a **Summary of Financial Needs.** This document is an **outline** giving the following information:

1. **Why** you are applying for a loan.

2. **How much** you need.

Note: A sample Summary of Financial Needs follows on the facing page.

Sample Page of a Summary of Financial Needs

Summary of Financial Needs

I.   ABC Corporation is seeking a loan to increase growth capital in the following areas of production:

   A.   Equipment (new and more modern)

   B.   Training of personnel in operation of above

II.   Funds needed to accomplish above goal will be $100,000.

   A.   See "Loan Fund Dispersal Statement" for distribution of funds and back-up statement.

LOAN FUND DISPERSAL STATEMENT

USES OF FINANCING - The potential lender will require a statement of how the money you intend to borrow will be used. It will be necessary for you to tell:

1. **How** you intend to utilize the loan funds.

2. **Back up your statement** with supporting data.

Note: The latter will show the lender that you have done your homework properly.

The following are two examples of what we mean:

EXAMPLE 1:

> **How Money Will Be Used:** Funds for advertising.
>
> **Back-Up Statement:** Refer to the advertising section of your plan. That section must contain a breakdown of how you intend to do your advertising. Rate sheets should be included in the Supporting Documents.

EXAMPLE 2:

> **How Money Will Be Used:** Funds for expansion. Include a concise statement explaining how you intend to expand.
>
> **Back-Up Statement:** Include the following information:
>
> a. Projected costs of carrying out plans.
>
> b. Projections as to how that expansion will ultimately result in in creased profits for your business and thereby enable you to repay your loan.
>
> c. References to other sections of your business plan that relate to projected expansion.

Note: A sample **Loan Fund Dispersal Statement** has been included for your convenience.

You must be sure that your supporting data can be easily found by the loan officer who is examining your application. If your information is not well-organized and easily retrievable, you will risk having your loan turned down simply because information cannot be located. The necessity of having a well-written Table of Contents will be discussed in Chapter 10, "Putting Your Plan Together."

Sample Page of Loan Fund Dispersal Statement

Loan Fund Dispersal Statement

1. DISPERSAL OF LOAN FUNDS

ABC Corporation will utilize anticipated loan funds in the amount of $100,000 to modernize its production equipment. This will necessitate the purchase of two new pieces of equipment and the training of present personnel in the operation of that equipment.

2. BACK-UP STATEMENT

   a. The equipment needed is as follows:

      (1) High-speed F-34 Atlas Press (purchase price: $65,000)

      (2) S71 Jaworski Ebber (purchase price: $18,000)

   b. The training is available from the manufacturer as a three-week intensive program. (cost: 10 employees @ $1,200 = $12,000)

   c. The remaining $5,000 of loan funds will be used to make the first monthly installment on loan repayment—a period of low production due to employee training off the premises.

   d. The equipment will result in a 35% increase in production and will decrease unit cost by 25%. The end result will be a net profit increase sufficient to repay the loan and interest within three years with a profit margin of 15%.*

* Note: Refer to page 17 for production plan of ABC Corporation. See pages 27 and 28 of the marketing section for market research and projected trends in the industry. (See footnote at bottom of page.)

Page numbers in the example above are hypothetical and do not refer to page numbers in this book.

When writing your Business Plan, be sure that your production plan includes a description of the equipment, how the work will be done, by whom and at what cost.

The market research will show projected demand for your product, and thus will show how increased production will result in increased sales and ultimately in your company's capability to repay the loan.

Pro Forma Statements

The financial statements that follow are pro forma statements. They show your projections for the future profitability of your business.

All business plans must contain the following pro forma statements:

Cash Flow Statement

Three-Year Income Projection

Break-Even Analysis

Also included in this section are:

- **"Cash to be Paid Out"** and **"Sources of Cash"** worksheets. They will help you to develop your cash flow statement and should be included in your business plan.

- A **"Quarterly Budget Analysis"** form. This is your tool for comparing the projections for your company with its actual performance. Your cash flow statement will be effective only if it is revised quarterly reflecting the results of a budget analysis.

Note: If you are a new business, you have no actual performance to measure against projections. Therefore, you will not have a quarterly budget analysis until you have been in business for three months.

If you have been in business for one or more quarters, do a quarterly budget analysis, revise your cash flow statement accordingly and insert the revised cash flow statement in your business plan.

PRO FORMA CASH FLOW STATEMENT (SAME AS BUDGET)

It is a fact that a third or more of today's businesses fail due to a lack of cash flow. The cash flow statement is usually the first thing a lender or investor examines in your business plan. What is cash flow?

WHAT IS A CASH FLOW STATEMENT?

This is the document that **projects** what your Business Plan means in terms of dollars. A cash flow statement is the same as a budget. It is a pro forma (or projected) statement used for internal planning and estimates how much money will flow into and out of a business during a designated period of time, usually the coming tax year. Your profit at the end of the year will depend on the proper balance between cash inflow and outflow.

The Cash Flow Statement identifies when cash is expected to be received and when it must be spent to pay bills and debts. It also allows the manager to identify where the necessary cash will come from.

This statement deals only with **actual cash transactions** and not with depreciation and amortization of goodwill or other noncash expense items. Expenses are paid from cash on hand, sale of assets, revenues from sales and services, interest earned on investments, money borrowed from a lender and influx of capital in exchange for equity in the company. If your business will require $100,000 to pay its expenses and $50,000 to support the owners, you will need at least an equal amount of money flowing into the business just to maintain the status quo. Anything less will eventually lead to an inability to pay your creditors or yourself.

The availability or nonavailability of cash **when** it is needed for expenditures gets to the very heart of the matter. By careful planning, you must try to project not only **how much** cash will have to flow into and out of your business, but also **when** it will need to flow in and out. A business may be able to plan for gross receipts that will cover its needs. However, if those sales do not take place in time to pay the expenses, your venture will soon be history unless you plan ahead for other sources of cash to tide the business over until the revenues are realized.

Time Period. The Cash Flow Statement should be prepared on a monthly basis for the next tax year of your business. To be effective, it must be analyzed and revised quarterly to reflect actual performance in the preceding three months of operations.

TO HELP PREPARE YOUR CASH FLOW STATEMENT

Before preparing your budget, it might be useful to compile individual projections and budgets. They might be as follows:

- **Revenue Projections (Product and Service)**

- **Inventory Purchases**

- **Variable (Selling, Direct) Expense Budget (w/Marketing Budget)**

- **Fixed (Administrative, Indirect) Expense Budget**

PRE-PLANNING WORKSHEETS

Because the cash flow statement deals with cash inflow and cash outflow, the first step in planning can be best accomplished by preparing two worksheets.

1. **Cash to be Paid Out**

   This worksheet documents the cash flowing out of your business. It identifies categories of expenses and obligations and the projected amount of cash needed in each category. Use the information from your individual budgets (inventory purchases, direct expenses, administrative expenses, owner draws, etc.).

   These expenditures are not always easy to estimate. If yours is a new business, it will be necessary for you to do lots of market research. If you are an existing business, you will combine information from past financial statements with trends in your particular industry.

2. **Sources of Cash**

   Use this worksheet to document the cash flowing into your business. It will help you to estimate how much cash will be available from what sources. To complete this worksheet, you will have to look at cash on hand, projected revenues, assets that can be liquidated, possible lenders or investors and owner equity to be contributed. This worksheet will force you to take a look at any existing possibilities for increasing available cash.

Sample Worksheets

On the next four pages, you will find examples of the two worksheets along with accompanying information explaining each of the categories used. The worksheets are filled in for our fictitious company, **ABC Company**, to help you understand the process.

Please note that the Cash to be Paid Out Worksheet shows a need for $131,000. It was necessary in projecting Sources of Cash to account for $131,000 without the projected sales because payment is not expected to be received until November and December (too late for cash needs January through October). Next year, those revenues will be reflected in cash on hand or other salable assets.

Be sure to figure all estimates on both your worksheets for the same period of time (annually, quarterly, monthly).

Note: Blank forms of these two worksheets are provided in Appendix III.

EXPLANATION OF CATEGORIES

CASH TO BE PAID OUT WORKSHEET

1. START-UP COSTS

These are the costs incurred by you to get your business underway. They are generally one-time expenses and are capitalized for tax purposes.

2. INVENTORY PURCHASES

Cash to be spent during the period on items intended for resale. If you purchase manufactured products, this includes the cash outlay for those purchases. If you are the manufacturer, include labor and materials on units to be produced.

3. VARIABLE EXPENSES (Selling or Direct Expenses)

These are the costs of all expenses that will relate directly to your product or service (other than manufacturing costs or purchase price of inventory).

4. FIXED EXPENSES (Administrative or Indirect Expenses)

Include all expected costs of office overhead. If certain bills must be paid ahead, include total cash outlay even if covered period extends into the next year.

5. ASSETS (Long-Term Purchases)

These are the capital assets that will be depreciated over a period of years (land, buildings, vehicles, equipment). Determine how you intend to pay for them and include all cash to be paid out in the current period.

6. LIABILITIES

What are the payments you expect to have to make to retire any debts or loans? Do you have any Accounts Payable as you begin the new year? You will need to determine the amount of cash outlay that needs to be paid in the current year. If you have a car loan for $20,000 and you pay $500 per month for 12 months, you will have a cash outlay of $6,000 for the coming year.

7. OWNER EQUITY

This item is frequently overlooked in planning cash flow. If you, as the business owner, will need a draw of $2,000 per month to live on, you must plan for $24,000 cash flowing out of your business. Failure to plan for it will result in a cash flow shortage and may cause your business to fail.

Note: *Be sure to use the same time period throughout your worksheet.*

ABC COMPANY
CASH TO BE PAID OUT WORKSHEET
(Cash Flowing Out Of The Business)

1. START-UP COSTS

Business License		$ 30.00
Corporation Filing		500.00
Legal Fees		920.00
Other start-up costs:		

2. INVENTORY PURCHASES

Cash out for goods intended for resale	32,000.00

3. VARIABLE EXPENSES (SELLING/DIRECT)

Advertising/Marketing	8,000.00	
Freight	2,500.00	
Fulfillment	800.00	
Packaging costs	Ø	
Sales Salaries/Commissions	14,000.00	
Travel	1,550.00	
Miscellaneous	300.00	
TOTAL SELLING EXPENSES		27,150.00

4. FIXED EXPENSES (ADMINISTRATIVE/INDIRECT)

Financial Administration	1,800.00	
Insurance	900.00	
Licenses and Permits	100.00	
Office Salaries	16,300.00	
Rent Expense	8,600.00	
Utilities	2,400.00	
Miscell. Fixed Expense	400.00	
TOTAL OPERATING EXPENSE		30,500.00

5. ASSETS (LONG-TERM PURCHASES)

Cash to be paid out in current period	6,000.00

6. LIABILITIES

Cash outlay for retiring debts, loans and/or accounts payable	9,900.00

7. OWNER EQUITY

Cash to be withdrawn by owner	24,000.00

TOTAL CASH TO BE PAID OUT $ 131,000.00

EXPLANATION OF CATEGORIES
SOURCES OF CASH WORKSHEET

1. CASH ON HAND

Money that you have on hand. Be sure to include petty cash and monies not yet deposited.

2. SALES (REVENUES)

This includes projected revenues from the sale of your product and/ or service. If payment is not expected during the time period covered by this worksheet, do not include that portion of your sales. Think about the projected timing of sales. If receipts will be delayed beyond the time when a large amount of cash is needed, make a notation to that effect and take it into consideration when determining the need for temporary financing. Include deposits you require on expected sales or services. When figuring collections on Accounts Receivable, you will have to project the percentage of invoices that will be lost to bad debts and subtract it from your Accounts Receivable total.

3. MISCELLANEOUS INCOME

Do you, or will you have, any monies out on loan or deposited in accounts that will yield interest income during the period in question?

4. SALE OF LONG-TERM ASSETS

If you are expecting to sell any of your fixed assets such as land, buildings, vehicles, machinery, equipment, etc., be sure to include only the cash you will receive during the current period.

Important: At this point in your worksheet, add up all sources of cash. If you do not have an amount equal to your projected needs, you will have to plan sources of cash covered under numbers 5 and 6.

5. LIABILITIES

This figure represents the amount you will be able to borrow from lending institutions such as banks, finance companies, the SBA, etc. Be reasonable about what you think you can borrow. If you have no collateral, have no business plan, or if you have a poor financial history, you will find it difficult, if not impossible, to find a lender. This source of cash requires **preplanning.**

6. EQUITY

Sources of equity come from owner investments, contributed capital, sale of stock or venture capital. Do you anticipate the availability of personal funds? Does your business have the potential for growth that might interest a venture capitalist? Be sure to be realistic in this area. You cannot sell stock (or equity) to a nonexistent investor.

ABC COMPANY
SOURCES OF CASH WORKSHEET
(Cash Flowing Into The Business)

1. CASH ON HAND $ __20,000.00__

2. SALES (REVENUES)

Sales Income*   ** Most of this sales revenue will not be received until November or December.*   90,000.00

Services Income   22,000.00

Deposits on Sales or Services   Ø

Collections on Accounts Receivable   3,000.00

3. MISCELLANEOUS INCOME

Interest Income   1,000.00

Payments to be Received on Loans   Ø

4. SALE OF LONG-TERM ASSETS   Ø

5. LIABILITIES   40,000.00

Loan Funds (To be received during period
from banks, SBA and other lending institutions)

6. EQUITY

Owner Investments (Sole Prop/Partners)   *(from C.D.)*   10,000.00

Contributed Capital (Corporation)

Sale of Stock (Corporation)

Venture Capital   35,000.00

TOTAL CASH AVAILABLE: **A.** *Without Sales* $ **131,000.00**

   B. *With Sales* $ **221,000.00**

USING THE WORKSHEETS: Now that you have completed the two worksheets, you are ready to use that information. You have estimated **how much** cash will be needed for the year and you now know what sources are available. In the next phase of cash flow planning you will break the time period of one year into monthly segments and predict **when** the cash will be needed to make the financial year flow smoothly.

Project sales on a monthly basis based on payment of invoices, demand for your particular product or service and ability to fill that demand. Figure the cost of goods, fixed and variable expenses in monthly increments. Most will vary. When do you plan to purchase the most inventory? What months will require the most advertising? Are you expecting a rent or insurance increase? When will commissions be due on expected sales. Determine your depreciable assets needs. How much will the payments be and when will they begin? Fill in as much of the cash flow statement as you can using those projections and any others that you can comfortably determine.

To clarify the process of filling in a cash flow statement, we will walk you through January and February again using ABC Company as our example.

JANUARY PROJECTIONS
1. ABC projects a beginning cash balance of $20,000.
2. Cash Receipts: Product manufacturing will not be completed until February, so there will be no sales. However, service income of $4,000 is projected.
3. Interest on the $20,000 will amount to about $100 at current rate.
4. There are no long-term assets to sell. Enter a zero.
5. Adding 1,2,3 and 4 the Total Cash Available will be $24,100.
6. Cash Payments: Product will be available from manufacturer in February and payment will not be due until pickup. However, there will be proto-type costs of $5,000.
7. Variable Expenses: Estimated at $1,140.
8. Fixed Expenses: Estimated at $1,215.
9. Interest Expense: No outstanding debts or loans. Enter zero.
10. Taxes: No profit for previous quarter. No estimated taxes would be due.
11. Payments on Long-Term Assets: ABC plans to purchase office equipment to be paid in full at the time of purchase. Enter $1139.
12. Loan Repayments: No loans have been received. Enter zero.
13. Owner Draws: Owner will need $2,000 for living expenses.
14. Total Cash Paid Out: Add 6 through 13. Total $10,494.
15. Cash Balance: Subtract Cash Paid Out from Total Cash Available ($13,606).
16. Loans to be Received: Being aware of the $30,000 to be paid to the manufacturer in February, a loan of $40,000 is anticipated to increase Cash Available. (This requires advance planning.)
17. Equity Deposit: Owner plans to add $5,000 from personal CD.
18. Ending Cash Balance: Adding 15, 16 and 17 the sum is $58,606.

FEBRUARY PROJECTIONS
1. February Beginning Cash Balance: January Ending Cash Balance ($58,606).
2. Cash Receipts: Still no sales, but service income is $2,000.
3. Interest Income: Projected at about $120.
4. Sale of Long-Term Assets: None. Enter zero.
5. Total Cash Available: Add 1,2,3 and 4. The result is $60,726.
6. Cash Payments: $30,000 due to manufacturer, $400 due on packaging design.
7. Continue as in January. Don't forget to include payments on your loan.

ABC COMPANY
Partial Cash Flow Statement

	JAN	FEB
BEGINNING CASH BALANCE	$ 20,000	$ 58,606
CASH RECEIPTS		
a. Sales revenues (Cash sales)	4,000	2,000
b. Receivables to be collected	Ø	Ø
c. Interest income	100	120
d. Sale of long-term assets	Ø	Ø
TOTAL CASH AVAILABLE	24,100	60,726
CASH PAYMENTS		
a. Cost of goods to be sold		
1. Purchases	Ø	30,000
2. Material	Ø	Ø
3. Labor	5,000	400
b. Variable expenses (Selling, Direct)		
1. Advertising/Marketing	300	
2. Freight	120	
3. Fulfillment	Ø	
4. Packaging Costs	270	
5. Sales Salaries/Commissions	Ø	
6. Travel	285	CONT. as in JAN.
7. Miscellaneous	165	
c. Fixed expenses (Administrative, Indirect)		
1. Financial Admin.	80	
2. Insurance	125	
3. Licenses and permits	200	
4. Office salaries	500	
5. Rent expenses	110	
6. Utilities	200	
7. Miscellaneous fixed expenses	Ø	
d. Interest expense	Ø	
e. Federal income tax	Ø	
f. Other uses	Ø	
g. Payments on long-term assets	1,139	
h. Loan Payment	Ø	
i. Owner draws	2,000	
TOTAL CASH PAID OUT	10,494	
CASH BALANCE/DEFICIENCY	13,606	
LOANS TO BE RECEIVED	40,000	
EQUITY DEPOSITS	5,000	
ENDING CASH BALANCE	$ 58,606	

DIRECTIONS FOR

COMPLETING YOUR CASH FLOW STATEMENT

This page contains instructions for completing the cash flow statement on the next page. A blank form for your own projections can be found in Appendix III.

1. **VERTICAL COLUMNS** are divided into the twelve months and preceded by a "Total Column."

2. **HORIZONTAL POSITIONS** on the statement contain all the sources of cash and cash to be paid out. These figures are retrieved from the two previous worksheets and from individual budgets.

Figures are projected for each month, reflecting the flow of cash in and out of your business for a one-year period. Begin with the first month of your business cycle (January in this example) and proceed as follows:

1. Project the Beginning Cash Balance. Enter under "January."

2. Project the Cash Receipts for January.

3. Add Beginning Cash Balance and Cash Receipts to determine Total Cash Available.

4. Project the Variable, Fixed and Interest Expenses for January.

5. Project monies due on Taxes, Long-Term Assets and Loan Repayments. Also project any amounts to be drawn by owners.

6. Total all Expenses and Draws. This is Total Cash Paid Out.

7. Subtract Total Cash Paid Out from Total Cash Available. The result is entered under "Cash Balance/Deficiency." Be sure to bracket this figure if the result is a negative to avoid errors.

8. Project Loans to be Received and Equity Deposits to be made. Add to Cash Balance/Deficiency to get Ending Cash Balance.

9. The Ending Cash Balance for January is carried forward and becomes February's Beginning Cash Balance.

10. The process is repeated until December is completed.

TO COMPLETE THE "TOTAL COLUMN":

1. The Beginning Cash Balance for January is entered in the first space of the "Total" column.

2. The monthly figures for each category are added horizontally and the result entered in the corresponding Total category.

3. The Total column is computed in the same manner as each of the individual months. If you have been accurate in your computations, the December Ending Cash Balance will be exactly the same as the Total Ending Cash Balance.

Note: If your business is new, you will have to base your projections solely on market research and industry trends. If you have an established business, you will also use your financial statements from previous years.

PRO FORMA CASH FLOW STATEMENT

Company Name: _____

FOR THE YEAR 19____	TOTAL	JAN	FEB	MAR	APR	MAY	JUN	JUL	AUG	SEP	OCT	NOV	DEC
BEGINNING CASH BALANCE													
CASH RECEIPTS													
a. Sales revenues (Cash sales)													
b. Receivables to be collected													
c. Interest income													
d. Sale of long-term assets													
TOTAL CASH AVAILABLE													
CASH PAYMENTS													
a. Cost of goods to be sold													
1. Purchases													
2. Material													
3. Labor													
b. Variable expenses (Selling, Direct)													
1. Advertising/Marketing													
2. Freight													
3. Fulfillment													
4. Packaging costs													
5. Sales Salaries/Commissions													
6. Travel													
7. Miscellaneous Variable Expenses													
c. Fixed expenses (Administrative, Indirect)													
1. Financial Admin.													
2. Insurance													
3. Licenses and permits													
4. Office salaries													
5. Rent expenses													
6. Utilities													
7. Miscellaneous Fixed Expenses													
d. Interest expense													
e. Federal income tax													
f. Other uses													
g. Payments on long-term assets													
h. Loan Payment													
i. Owner draws													
TOTAL CASH PAID OUT													
CASH BALANCE/DEFICIENCY													
LOANS TO BE RECEIVED													
EQUITY DEPOSITS													
ENDING CASH BALANCE													

This is the extension of the form found on page 59. A blank form is located in the Appendix for your use. Variable and fixed expenses categories have not been named. Customize them for your business.

QUARTERLY BUDGET ANALYSIS

YEARLY BUDGET. The same as the Pro Forma Cash Flow Statement discussed on the preceding pages. It is of no value to you as a business owner unless there is some means to evaluate the actual performance of your company and measure it against your projections.

QUARTERLY BUDGET ANALYSIS. The record that is used to compare your projected cash flow statement (or budget) with your business's actual performance. Its purpose is to let you know whether or not you are operating within your projections and to help you maintain control of all phases of your business operations. When your analysis shows that you are over or under budget in any area, it will be necessary to determine the reason for the deviation and implement changes for the future that will enable you to get back on track.

Example: If you have budgeted $1,000 in advertising funds for the first quarter and you find that you have actually spent $1,600, the first thing you should do is look at the sales that have occurred as a result of increased advertising. If they are over projections by an amount equal to or more than the $600, your budget will still be in good shape. If not, you will have to find expenses in your budget that can be revised to make up the deficit. You might be able to take a smaller draw for yourself or spend less on travel. You might even be able to increase your profits by adding a new product or service.

It should be clear at this point that the correct process to keep you from running out of operating capital in the middle of the year is to make yearly projections, analyze at the end of each quarter and then to revise your budget based on that analysis and current industry trends.

HOW TO DEVELOP A QUARTERLY BUDGET ANALYSIS

There is a blank form for your use in Appendix III. The Quarterly Budget Analysis needs the following seven columns:

1. **Budget Item:** The list of budget items is taken from headings on the Pro Forma Cash Flow Statement. All items in your budget should be listed.
2. **Budget This Quarter:** Fill in the amount budgeted for current quarter from your Pro Forma Cash Flow Statement.
3. **Actual This Quarter:** Fill in actual expenditures or receipts for quarter.
4. **Variation This Quarter:** Amount spent or received over or under budget.
5. **Year-To-Date Budget:** Amount budgeted from beginning of year through and including current quarter (from cash flow statement).
6. **Actual Year-To-Date:** Actual amount spent or received from beginning of year through current quarter.
7. **Variation Year-To-Date:** Subtract the amount spent or received from the amount budgeted from the start of the year through the current quarter.

ABC COMPANY
QUARTERLY BUDGET ANALYSIS

All items contained in the Budget are listed on this form. The second column is the amount budgeted for the current quarter. By subtracting the amount actually spent, you will arrive at the Variation for the Quarter. The last three columns are for year-to-date figures. If you analyze at the end of the 3rd Quarter, figures will represent the first nine months of the tax year.

Making Calculations: When you calculate variations, the amounts are preceded by either a plus (+) or a minus (-), depending on whether the category is a revenue (income) or an expense. If the actual amount is greater than the amount budgeted, (1) Revenue categories will represent the variation as a positive (+); (2) Expense categories will represent the variation as a negative (-).

For the Quarter Ending _Sept. 30_ , 19 _93_ . **YTD = year-to-date**

BUDGET ITEM	BUDGET THIS QUARTER	ACTUAL THIS QUARTER	VARIATION THIS QUARTER	YTD BUDGET	ACTUAL YTD	VARIATION YTD
SALES REVENUES	145,000	150,000	+5,000	400,000	410,000	+10,000
Less Cost of Goods	80,000	82,500	-2,500	240,000	243,000	-3,000
GROSS PROFIT	65,000	67,500	+2,500	160,000	167,000	+7,000
VARIABLE EXPENSES						
1. Advert/Mktg	3,000	3,400	-400	6,000	6,200	-200
2. Freight	6,500	5,750	+750	16,500	16,350	+150
3. Fulfillment	1,400	950	+450	3,800	4,100	-300
4. Packaging	750	990	-240	2,200	2,300	-100
5. Salaries/Commissions	6,250	6,250	Ø	18,750	18,750	Ø
6. Travel	500	160	+340	1,500	1,230	+270
7. Miscellaneous	Ø	475	-475	Ø	675	-675
FIXED EXPENSES						
1. Financial Admin.	1,500	1,500	Ø	4,500	4,700	-200
2. Insurance	2,250	2,250	Ø	6,750	6,750	Ø
3. Licenses & Permits	1,000	600	+400	3,500	3,400	+100
4. Office Salaries	1,500	1,500	Ø	4,500	4,500	Ø
5. Rent	3,500	3,500	Ø	10,500	10,500	Ø
6. Utilities	750	990	-240	2,250	2,570	-320
7. Miscellaneous	Ø	60	-60	Ø	80	-80
NET INCOME FROM OPERATIONS	36,100	39,125	+3,025	79,250	84,895	+5,645
INTEREST INCOME	1,250	1,125	-125	3,750	3,700	-50
INTEREST EXPENSE	1,500	1,425	+75	4,500	4,500	Ø
NET PROFIT (LOSS) BEFORE TAXES	35,850	38,825	2,975	78,500	84,095	+5,595
TAXES	8,500	9,500	-1,000	25,500	28,500	-3,000
NET PROFIT (LOSS) AFTER TAXES	27,350	29,325	+1,975	53,000	55,595	+2,595
NON-INCOME STATEMENT ITEMS						
1. L-Term Asset Repay'ts	2,400	3,400	-1,000	7,200	8,200	-1,000
2. Loan Repayments	3,400	3,400	Ø	8,800	8,800	Ø
3. Owner Draws	6,000	6,900	-900	18,000	18,900	-900

BUDGET DEVIATIONS	Current Quarter	Year-To-Date
1. Income Statement Items:	$ +1,975	$ +2,595
2. Non-Income Statement Items:	$ -1,900	$ -1,900
3. Total Deviation (1+2)	$ +75	$ +695

THREE-YEAR INCOME PROJECTION

WHAT IS A THREE-YEAR INCOME PROJECTION?

A three-year income projection is a pro forma income (or profit & loss) statement. This statement differs from a cash flow statement in that it includes only projected income and deductible expenses. This difference is illustrated as follows: Your company will make payments of $9000 on a vehicle in 1994. Interest amounted to $3,000. The full amount ($9,000) will be recorded on a cash flow statement; only the interest ($3,000) will be recorded on a projected income statement. Principal paid on your loan ($6,000) is not a deductible expense.

VARIATION IN PERIOD COVERED

There is some difference of opinion as to the period of time that should be covered and whether or not it should be on an annual or month-by-month basis. If you are seeking funds, talk to the lender about his or her specific requirements. If not, we suggest a three-year projection with annual rather than monthly projections. With the rapidly-changing economy, it is difficult to make accurate detailed projections.

ACCOUNT FOR INCREASES AND DECREASES

Increases in income and expenses are to be expected and should be reflected in your projections. Industry trends can also cause decreases in both income and expenses. An example of this might be in the computer industry where heavy competition and standardization of components have caused a decrease in both cost and sale price of certain items. The state of the economy will also be a contributing factor in the outlook for your business.

SOURCES OF INFORMATION

Information for a three-year projection can be developed from your pro forma cash flow statement and your business and marketing analysis. The first year's figures can be transferred from the totals of income and expense items. The second and third years' figures are derived by combining these totals with projected trends in your particular industry. Again, if you are an established business, you will also be able to use past financial statements to help you determine what you project for the future of your business. Be sure to take into account fluctuations anticipated in costs, efficiency of operation, changes in your market, etc.

FOR YOUR OWN USE

A sample of a Three-Year Income Projection form is provided on the next page. A blank form is located in Appendix III. If you prefer, it can be compiled on a month-by-month basis and then compared with actual monthly performance. If prepared in this manner, your projection statement can provide an annual projection for your next business year.

ABC COMPANY
THREE-YEAR INCOME PROJECTION

FOR THE YEARS 19 _93_ , 19 _94_ AND 19 _95_ .

	YEAR 1	YEAR 2	YEAR 3
INCOME			
1. NET SALES (Gross less ret. & allow.)	500,000	540,000	595,000
2. COST OF GOODS SOLD (c. minus d.)	312,000	330,000	365,000
a. Beginning Inventory	147,000	155,000	175,000
b. Purchases	320,000	350,000	375,000
c. C.O.G. Available for Sale (a+b)	467,000	505,000	550,000
d. Less End. Inv. (Dec. 31st)	155,000	175,000	185,000
3. GROSS PROFIT ON SALES (1 minus 2)	188,000	210,000	230,000
EXPENSES			
1. VARIABLE (Selling/Direct) (a. thru h.)			
a. Advertising/Marketing	9,000	12,000	12,000
b. Freight	22,000	25,500	26,500
c. Fulfillment	2,000	4,000	4,000
d. Packaging Costs	3,000	2,800	2,900
e. Salaries/Wages/Commissions	25,000	35,000	40,000
f. Travel	5,000	5,000	4,500
g. Miscellaneous Selling Exp.			
h. Depreciation (Product/Services Assets)			
2. FIXED (Administrative/Indirect) (a. thru h.)			
a. Insurance	9,000	9,000	9,000
b. Licenses & Permits	4,000	4,000	4,000
c. Office Salaries	16,000	16,000	16,800
d. Rent Expense	14,000	14,000	14,000
e. Financial Admin.	7,000	7,000	7,500
f. Utilities	3,000	3,500	4,000
g. Other Overhead			
h. Depreciation (Office Equipment)			
TOTAL OPERATING EXPENSES (Variable+Fixed)	119,000	137,800	145,200
NET INCOME FROM OPERATIONS (Gross Profit less Expenses)	69,000	72,200	84,800
OTHER INCOME (INTEREST)	+ 5,000	+ 5,000	+ 5,000
OTHER EXPENSE (INTEREST)	- 7,000	- 5,000	- 4,000
NET PROFIT (LOSS) BEFORE INCOME TAXES	67,000	72,200	85,800
TAXES (Federal, Self-Employment, State)	26,000	29,000	34,200
NET PROFIT (LOSS) AFTER TAXES	41,000	43,200	51,600

BREAK-EVEN ANALYSIS

WHAT IS A BREAK-EVEN POINT?

This is the point at which a company's costs exactly match the sales volume and at which the business has neither made a profit nor incurred a loss. The break-even point can be determined by mathematical calculation or by the development of a graph. It can be expressed in:

1. **Total Dollars of Revenue** (exactly offset by total costs).

    -or-

2. **Total Units of Production** (cost of which exactly equals the income derived by their sale).

To apply a break-even analysis to an operation, you will need three projections. They are as follows:

1. **Fixed Costs for the Period** (Administrative Overhead, Depreciation, Interest, etc.). Costs remain constant even during a slow period.

2. **Variable Costs** (Cost of Goods + Selling Expenses). Usually varies. The greater the sales volume, the higher the cost.

3. **Total Sales Volume** (Projected sales for same period).

SOURCE OF INFORMATION

All of your figures can be derived from your Three-Year Projection. By now you should be able to see that each financial document in your business plan builds on the ones done previously. Retrieve the figures and plug them into the following mathematical formula.

MATHEMATICALLY

A firm's sales at break-even point can be computed by using this formula:

B-E Point (Sales) = Fixed Costs + [(Variable Costs/Est.Revenues) x Sales]

Terms Used: a. Sales = volume of sales at Break-Even Point
              b. Fixed Costs = administrative expense, depreciation, interest
              c. Variable Costs = cost of goods and selling expenses
              d. Estimated Revenues = income (from sales of goods/services)

Example: a. S (Sales at B-E Point) = the unknown
              b. FC (Fixed Costs) = $25,000
              c. VC (Variable Costs) = $45,000
              d. R (Estimated Revenues) = $90,000

Using the formula, the computation would appear as follows:
$$S \text{ (at B-E Point)} = \$25,000 + [(\$45,000/\$90,000) \times S]$$
$$S = \$25,000 + (1/2 \times S)$$
$$S - 1/2\ S = \$25,000$$
$$1/2\ S = \$25,000$$
$$\mathbf{S = \$50,000} \text{ (Break-Even Point in terms of dollars of revenue exactly offset by total costs)}$$

GRAPHICALLY

Break-even point in graph form for the same business would be plotted as illustrated below. There is a blank form for your use in Appendix III.

BREAK-EVEN ANALYSIS GRAPH

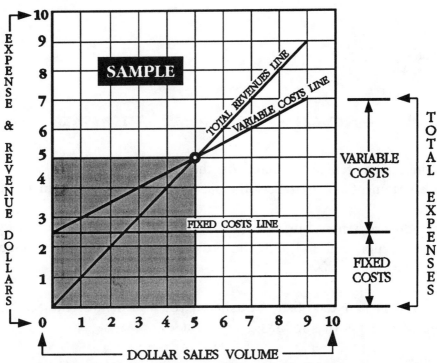

Note: Figures shown in tens of thousands of dollars. (Ex: 2 - $20,000)

TO COMPLETE THE GRAPH: Determine the following projections.

1. **Fixed Costs for Period:** Those costs that usually remain constant and must be met regardless of your sales volume (administrative, rent, insurance, depreciation, interest, salaries, etc.). **Ex: $25,000.**

2. **Variable Costs** - Cost associated with the production and selling of your products or services. If you have a product, you will include cost of goods (inventory purchases, labor, materials, freight, packaging, sales commissions, advertising, etc.). These costs may be expressed by multiplying the unit cost by the units to be sold for a product. **Example: $1.50 per unit x 30,000 units = $45,000; or for a service having no cost of goods, use total of projected selling expenses.**

3. **Total Sales Volume:** This is the figure representing units of product to be sold by sale price per unit. **Ex: 30,000 units @ $3.00 = $90,000;** for a service, multiply your billable hours by your hourly rate **(900 hours x $100 = $90,000).**

TO DRAW GRAPH LINES:

1. **Draw Horizontal Line** at point representing Fixed Costs (25).
2. **Draw Variable Cost Line** from left end of Fixed Cost Line sloping upward to point where Total Costs (Fixed + Variable) on vertical scale (7) meet Total Revenues on the horizontal scale (9).
3. **Draw Total Revenues Line** from zero through a point describing total Revenues on both scales (9).

BREAK-EVEN POINT. That point on the graph where the Variable Cost Line intersects the Total Revenue Line. This business estimates that it will break even at the time sales volume reaches $50,000. The triangular area below and to the left of that point represents company losses. The triangular area above and to the right of the point represents potential profit.

Actual Performance Statements

The financial statements covered on the following pages are actual performance statements. They reflect the activity of your business in the past.

If you are a new business owner, you have no business history. Your financial section will end with the projected statements and a Personal Financial History.

If you are an established business, you will include the actual performance statements that follow. They include:

Balance Sheet

Profit & Loss (Income) Statement

Business Financial History
or
Loan Application

BALANCE SHEET

WHAT IS A BALANCE SHEET?

The Balance Sheet is a financial statement that shows the financial position of the business as of a fixed date. It is usually done at the close of an accounting period. The Balance Sheet can be compared to a photograph. It is a picture of what your business owns and owes at a particular given moment and will show you whether your financial position is strong or weak. By regularly preparing this statement, you will be able to identify and analyze trends in the financial strength of your business and thus implement timely modifications.

ASSETS, LIABILITIES AND NET WORTH

All balance sheets are divided into three categories. The three are related in that at any given time, a business's assets equal the total contributions by its creditors and owners. They are defined as follows:

Assets = Anything your business owns that has monetary value

Liabilities = Debts owed by the business to any of its creditors

Net Worth (Capital) = An amount equal to the owner's equity

The relationship between these three terms is simply illustrated in a mathematical formula. It reads as follows:

$$\textbf{Assets - Liabilities = Net Worth}$$

Examined as such, it becomes apparent that if a business possesses more assets than it owes to creditors, its net worth will be a positive. Conversely, if the business owes more money to creditors than it possesses in assets, the net worth will be a negative.

CATEGORIES AND FORMAT

The Balance Sheet must follow an accepted accounting format and contain the previously-mentioned categories. By following this format, anyone reading the Balance Sheet can readily interpret it.

Note: A sample **Balance Sheet** and **Explanation of Categories** are provided for you on the next two pages. There is a blank form for your own use in Appendix III.

EXPLANATION OF CATEGORIES
BALANCE SHEET

ASSETS: Everything owned by or owed to your business that has cash value.

1. **Current Assets:** Assets that can be converted into cash within one year of the date on the Balance Sheet.

   a. **Cash:** Money you have on hand. Include monies not yet deposited.

   b. **Petty Cash:** Money deposited to Petty Cash & not yet expended.

   c. **Accounts Receivable:** Money owed to you for sale of goods and/or services.

   d. **Inventory:** Raw materials, work in process and goods manufactured or purchased for resale.

   e. **Short-Term Investments:** Expected to be converted to cash within one year—stocks, bonds, C.D.s. List at lesser of cost or market value.

   f. **Prepaid Expenses:** Goods or services purchased or rented prior to use (ex: rent, insurance, prepaid inventory purchases, etc.).

2. **Long-Term Investments:** Stocks, bonds, and special savings accounts to be kept for at least one year.

3. **Fixed Assets:** Resources a business owns and does not intend for resale.

   a. **Land:** List at original purchase price.

   b. **Buildings:** List at cost less depreciation.

   c. **Equipment, Furniture, Autos/Vehicles:** List at cost less depreciation. "Kelley Blue Book" can be used to determine value of vehicles.

LIABILITIES: What your business owes; claims by creditors on your assets.

1. **Current Liabilities:** Those obligations payable within one operating cycle.

   a. **Accounts Payable:** Obligations payable within one operating cycle.

   b. **Notes Payable:** Short-term notes; list the balance of principal due. Separately list the current portion of long-term debts.

   c. **Interest Payable:** Interest accrued on loans and credit.

   d. **Taxes Payable:** Amounts estimated to have been incurred during the accounting period.

   e. **Payroll Accrual:** Current Liabilities on salaries and wages.

2. **Long-Term Liabilities:** Outstanding balance less the current portion due (mortgage, vehicle, etc.).

NET WORTH: (Also called "Owner Equity"): The claims of the owner or owners on the assets of the business. (Document according to the legal structure of your business.)

1. **Proprietorship or Partnership:** Each owner's original investment plus earnings after withdrawals.

2. **Corporation:** The sum of contributions by owners or stockholders plus earnings retained after paying dividends.

ABC COMPANY
BALANCE SHEET

COMPANY NAME: ABC Company

Date: September 30, 19 93

ASSETS

Current Assets

Cash	$ 8,742
Petty Cash	$ 167
Accounts Receivable	$ 5,400
Inventory	$ 101,800
Short-Term Investments	$ Ø
Prepaid Expenses	$ 1,967

Long-Term Investments $ Ø

Fixed Assets

Land (valued at cost) $ 185,000

Buildings $ 143,000
1. Cost 171,600
2. Less Acc. Depr. 28,600

Improvements $ Ø
1. Cost
2. Less Acc. Depr.

Equipment $ 5,760
1. Cost 7,200
2. Less Acc. Depr. 1,440

Furniture $ 2,150
1. Cost 2,150
2. Less Acc. Depr. Ø

Autos/Vehicles $ 16,432
1. Cost 19,700
2. Less Acc. Depr. 3,268

Other Assets
1. $
2. $

TOTAL ASSETS $ 470,418

LIABILITIES

Current Liabilities

Accounts Payable	$ 2,893
Notes Payable	$ Ø
Interest Payable	$ 1,842

Taxes Payable
Fed. Inc. Tax $ 5,200
State Inc. Tax $ 1,025
Self-Emp. Tax $ 800
Sales Tax Accrual $ 2,130
Property Tax $ Ø
Payroll Accrual $ 4,700

Long-Term Liabilities
Notes Payable $ 196,700

TOTAL LIABILITIES $ 215,290

NET WORTH

Proprietorship $
or
Partnership
John Smith, 60% Equity $ 153,077
Mary Blake, 40% Equity $ 102,051
or
Corporation
Capital Stock $
Surplus Paid In $
Retained Earnings $

TOTAL NET WORTH $ 255,128

Assets - Liabilities = Net Worth

Total Liabilities and Equity will always be equal to Total Assets

PROFIT & LOSS (INCOME) STATEMENT

WHAT IS A PROFIT & LOSS (INCOME) STATEMENT?

This statement shows your business financial activity over a period of time, usually your tax year. In contrast to the Balance Sheet, which shows a picture of your business at a given moment, the Profit & Loss Statement (P & L) can be likened to a moving picture—showing what has happened in your business over a period of time. It is an excellent tool for assessing your business. You will be able to pick out weaknesses in your operation and plan ways to run your business more effectively, thereby increasing your profits. For example, you may find that some heavy advertising that you did in March did not effectively increase your sales. In following years, you may decide to utilize your advertising funds more effectively by using them at a time when there is increased customer spending taking place. In the same way, you might examine your Profit & Loss Statement to see what months have the heaviest sales volume and plan your inventory accordingly. Comparison of your P & Ls from several years will give you an even better picture of the trends in your business. Do not underestimate the value of this particular tool when planning your tactics.

HOW TO DEVELOP A PROFIT & LOSS STATEMENT

The Profit & Loss Statement (Income Statement) is compiled from actual business transactions, in contrast to pro forma statements, which are projections for future business periods. The P & L shows where your money has come from and where it was spent over a specific period of time. It should be prepared not only at the end of the fiscal year, but at the close of each business month. It is one of the two principal financial statements prepared from the ledgers and the records of a business. **Income and expense account balances** are used in the Profit & Loss Statement. The remaining asset, liability and capital information provides the figures for the Balance Sheet covered on the last three pages.

At the end of each month, the accounts in the General Ledger are balanced and closed. Balances from the revenue accounts (numbered 400-499) and the expense accounts (numbered 500-599) must be transferred to your Profit & Loss Statement.

If you use an accounting professional or have a good in-house software program, either should generate a Profit & Loss Statement and Balance Sheet for you at the end of every month as well as at the end of your tax year. Many small business owners set up their own set of manual books. If your general records are set up properly, the transfer of information should still be fairly simple as long as you understand what information is needed and which general records are to be used as sources.

FORMAT AND SOURCES OF INFORMATION

The Profit & Loss (or Income) Statement must also follow an accepted GAAP format and contain certain categories. The following is the correct format and a brief explanation of the items to be included or computations to be made in each category in order to arrive at "The Bottom Line" or owner's share of the profit for the period:

INCOME

1. **Net Sales (Gross sales less Returns and Allowances):** What were your cash receipts for the period? If your accounting is on an accrual basis, what amount did you invoice out during the period?

2. **Cost of Goods Sold:** See P & L form on p. 75 for computation.

3. **Gross Profit:** Subtract Cost of Goods from Net Sales.

EXPENSES

1. **Variable Expenses (Selling, Direct, Controllable):** What amounts did you actually spend on items directly related to your product or service (advertising, commissions, freight, etc.)?

2. **Administrative Expenses (Indirect, Fixed):** What amounts were spent during the period on office overhead (rent, insurance, accounting, office salaries, etc.)?

NET INCOME FROM OPERATIONS: Gross Profit minus Selling and Administrative Expenses.

   Other Income: Interest received during the period.
   Other Expense: Interest paid out during the period.

NET PROFIT (LOSS) BEFORE INCOME TAXES: The Net Income from Operations + Interest Income - Interest Expense

   Income Taxes: List income taxes paid out during the period (federal, state, self-employment).

NET PROFIT (LOSS) AFTER INCOME TAXES: Subtract all income taxes paid out from the net profit (or loss) before income taxes. This is what is known as "the bottom line."

SAMPLE FORMS

The next two pages contain two P & L forms. The first is divided into 12 months. At the end of the year, this form will provide an accurate picture of the year's financial activity. The second one (filled-in) is a form to be used for either a monthly or an annual Profit & Loss Statement. Blank forms are provided in Appendix III for your use.

PROFIT & LOSS STATEMENT (INCOME STATEMENT)

Company Name: _____

FOR THE YEAR 19____.	JAN	FEB	MAR	APR	MAY	JUN	JUL	AUG	SEP	OCT	NOV	DEC	YEAR TOTAL
INCOME													
1. NET SALES (Gross less ret. & allow.)													
2. COST OF GOODS SOLD (c. - d.)													
a. Beginning Inventory													
b. Purchases													
c. C.O.G. Available for Sale (a+b)													
d. Less End. Inv. (Dec. 31st)													
3. GROSS PROFIT ON SALES (1. minus 2.)													
EXPENSES													
1. VARIABLE (Selling/Direct Exp.) (a. thru h.)													
a. Advertising/Marketing													
b. Freight													
c. Fulfillment													
d. Packaging Costs													
e. Salaries/Wages/Commissions													
f. Travel													
g. Miscellaneous Selling Exp.													
h. Depreciation (Product/Service Assets)													
2. FIXED (Administrative/Indirect) (a. thru h.)													
a. Insurance													
b. Licenses & Permits													
c. Office Salaries													
d. Rent Expense													
e. Financial Admin.													
f. Utilities													
g. Other Overhead													
h. Depreciation (Office Equipment)													
TOTAL OPERATING EXPENSE (Variable+Fixed)													
NET INCOME FROM OPERATIONS (Gross Profit less Operating Expense)													
OTHER INCOME (INTEREST)													
OTHER EXPENSE (INTEREST)													
NET PROFIT (LOSS) BEFORE INCOME TAXES													
TAXES (Federal, Self-Employment, State)													
NET PROFIT (LOSS) AFTER TAXES													

This form should be filled out at the end of every month when you close and balance your books. A blank form for your use has been provided in the Appendix. The variable and fixed expense categories are not filled-in so they can be customized to match your own business.

ABC COMPANY
PROFIT & LOSS (INCOME) STATEMENT

For the period beginning _____ and ending _____

INCOME		
1. NET SALES (Gross less ret. & allow.)		$500,000
2. COST OF GOODS SOLD (c. minus d.)		312,000
a. Beginning Inventory	147,000	
b. Purchases	320,000	
c. C.O.G. Available for Sale (a+b)	467,000	
d. Less End. Inv. (Dec. 31st)	155,000	
3. GROSS PROFIT ON SALES (1 minus 2)		$188,000
EXPENSES		
1. VARIABLE (Direct/Selling) (a. thru h.)		67,000
a. Advertising/Marketing	9,000	
b. Freight	19,000	
c. Fulfillment	2,000	
d. Packaging Costs	3,000	
e. Salaries/Wages/Commissions	27,200	
f. Travel	1,800	
g. Miscellaneous Selling Exp.		
h. Depreciation (Product/Services Assets)	5,000	
2. FIXED (Indirect/Administrative) (a. thru h.)		53,000
a. Insurance	19,000	
b. Licenses & Permits	4,000	
c. Office Salaries	6,000	
d. Rent Expense	4,000	
e. Financial Admin.	14,700	
f. Utilities	3,000	
g. Other Overhead		
h. Depreciation (Office Equipment)	2,300	
TOTAL OPERATING EXPENSE (1 + 2)		120,000
NET INCOME FROM OPERATIONS (Gross Profit less Total Op.Exp.)		68,000
OTHER INCOME (INTEREST)		+ 5,000
OTHER EXPENSE (INTEREST)		- 6,000
NET PROFIT (LOSS) BEFORE INCOME TAXES		$67,000
TAXES (Federal, Self-Employment, State)		- 23,000
NET PROFIT (LOSS) AFTER TAXES		**$44,000**

BUSINESS FINANCIAL HISTORY

The business financial history is the last of the financial statements required in your business plan. It is a summary of financial information about your company from its start to the present.

IF YOURS IS A NEW BUSINESS

You will have only projections for your business. If you are applying for a loan, the lender will require a **Personal Financial History**. This will be of benefit in that it will show the manner in which you have conducted your personal business, an indicator of the probability of your succeeding in your business.

IF YOURS IS AN ESTABLISHED BUSINESS

The loan application and your Business Financial History are the same. When you indicate that you are interested in obtaining a business loan, the institution considering the loan will supply you with an application. The format may vary slightly. When you receive your loan application, be sure to review it and think about how you are going to answer each item. Answer **all** questions and by all means be certain your information is accurate and that it can be easily verified.

INFORMATION NEEDED AND SOURCES

As you fill out your Business Financial History (loan application), it should become immediately apparent why this is the last financial document to be completed. All of the information needed will have been compiled previously in earlier parts of your plan and in the financials you have already completed. To help you with your financial history, the following is a list of information most frequently required. We have also listed some of the sources you can refer to for that information:

1. **Assets, Liabilities, Net Worth:** You should recognize these three as balance sheet terms. You have already completed the Balance Sheet for your company and need only to go back to that record and bring the dollar amounts forward.

2. **Contingent Liabilities:** These are debts you may come to owe in the future (for example: default on a cosigned note or settlement of a pending lawsuit).

3. **Inventory Details:** Information is derived from your Inventory Record. Also, in the Organizational Plan you should already have a summary of your current policies and methods of evaluation.

4. **Profit & Loss Statement:** This is revenue and expense information. You will transfer the information from your Annual Profit & Loss (last statement completed) or from a compilation of several if required by the lender.

5. **Real Estate Holdings, Stocks and Bonds:** Refer back to your Organizational Plan. You may also have to go through your investment records for more comprehensive information.

6. **Legal Structure Information (Sole Proprietorship, Partnership or Corporation):** There are generally three separate schedules on the financial history, one for each form of legal structure. You will be required to fill out the one that is appropriate to your business. In the Organizational section, you will have covered two areas that will serve as the source of this information—Legal Structure and Management. Supporting Documents may also contain some of the information that you will need.

7. **Audit Information:** Refer back to the Organizational Plan under Recordkeeping. You may also be asked questions about other prospective lenders, whether you are seeking credit, who audits your books, and when they were last audited.

8. **Insurance Coverage:** You will be asked to provide detailed information on the amounts of different types coverage (i.e., merchandise, equipment, public liability, earthquake, auto, etc.). Your Organizational Plan should contain information on coverage that can be brought forth to the financial history.

BUSINESS FINANCIAL HISTORY FORM - On the next two pages you will find an example of a Business Financial History that might be required by a potential lender or investor.

PERSONAL FINANCIAL STATEMENT FORM - If you are a new business and need your Personal Financial Statement for this section, you will find a sample form in Chapter 7, "Supporting Documents."

BUSINESS
FINANCIAL HISTORY

FINANCIAL STATEMENT
INDIVIDUAL, PARTNERSHIP, OR CORPORATION

FINANCIAL STATEMENT OF

NAME_____

ADDRESS_____

RECEIVED AT_____BRANCH

BUSINESS_____

AT CLOSE OF BUSINESS_____19___

To

The undersigned, for the purpose of procuring and establishing credit from time to time with you and to induce you to permit the undersigned to become indebted to you on notes, endorsements, guarantees, overdrafts or otherwise, furnishes the following (or in lieu thereof the attached, which is the most recent statement prepared by or for the undersigned) as being a full, true and correct statement of the financial condition of the undersigned on the date indicated, and agrees to notify you immediately of the extent and character of any material change in said financial condition, and also agrees that if the undersigned, or any endorser or guarantor of any of the obligations of the undersigned, at any time fails in business or becomes insolvent, or commits an act of bankruptcy, or if any deposit account of the undersigned with you, or any other property of the undersigned held by you, be attempted to be obtained or held by writ of execution, garnishment, attachment or other legal process, or if any of the representations made below prove to be untrue, or if the undersigned fails to notify you of any material change as above agreed, or if the business, or any interest therein, of the undersigned is sold, then and in such case, at your option, all of the obligations of the undersigned to you, or held by you, shall immediately become due and payable, without demand or notice. This statement shall be construed by you to be a continuing statement of the condition of the undersigned, and a new and original statement of all assets and liabilities upon each and every transaction in and by which the undersigned hereafter becomes indebted to you, until the undersigned advises in writing to the contrary.

ASSETS	DOLLARS	CENTS	LIABILITIES	DOLLARS	CENTS
Cash In_____ (NAME OF BANK)			Notes Payable to Banks_____		
Cash on Hand_____			Notes Payable and Trade Acceptances for Merchandise____		
Notes Receivable and Trade Acceptance (Includes $_____ Past Due)			Notes Payable to Others_____		
Accounts Receivable—$_____Less Reserves $_____			Accounts Payable (Includes $_____Past Due)		
Customer's . . . (Includes $_____Past Due)			Due to Partners, Employes, Relatives, Officers, Stockholders or Allied Companies		
Merchandise—Finished—How Valued____			Chattel Mortgages and Contracts Payable (Describe Monthly Payments) . . . . $_____		
Merchandise—Unfinished—How Valued____			Federal and State Income Tax____		
Merchandise—Raw Material—How Valued____			Accrued Liabilities (Interest, Wages, Taxes, Etc.)____		
Supplies on Hand____			Portion of Long Term Debt Due Within One Year____		
Stocks and Bonds—Listed (See Schedule B)____					
TOTAL CURRENT ASSETS			**TOTAL CURRENT LIABILITIES**		
Real Estate—Less Depreciation of: $_____Net (See Schedule A)			Liens on Real Estate (See Schedule A) $_____		
Machinery and Fixtures— Less Depreciation of: $_____Net			Less Current Portion Included Above $_____Net		
Automobiles and Trucks— Less Depreciation of: $_____Net			Capital Stock—Preferred____		
Stocks and Bonds—Unlisted (See Schedule B)____			Capital Stock—Common____		
Due from Partners, Employes, Relatives, Officers, Stockholders or Allied Companies____			Surplus—Paid In____		
Cash Value Life Insurance____			Surplus—Earned and Undivided Profits____		
Other Assets (Describe)____			Net Worth (If Not Incorporated)____		
TOTAL			**TOTAL**		

PROFIT AND LOSS STATEMENT FOR THE PERIOD FROM_____TO_____			CONTINGENT LIABILITIES (NOT INCLUDED ABOVE)		
Net Sales (After Returned Sales and Allowances)____			As Guarantor or Endorser____		
Cost of Sales:			Accounts, Notes, or Trade Acceptances Discounted or Pledged____		
Beginning Inventory			Surety On Bonds or Other Continent Liability____		
Purchases (or cost of goods mfd.)			Letters of Credit____		
TOTAL			Judgments Unsatisfied or Suits Pending____		
Less: Closing Inventory			Merchandise Commitments and Unfinished Contracts____		
Gross Profit on Sales			Merchandise Held On Consignment From Others____		
			Unsatisfied Tax Liens or Notices From the Federal or State Governments of Intention to Assess Such Liens____		
Operating Expenses:			**RECONCILEMENT OF NET WORTH OR EARNED SURPLUS**		
Salaries—Officers or Partners					
Salaries and Wages—Other			Net Worth or Earned Surplus at Beginning of Period____		
Rent			Add Net Profit or Deduct Net Loss____		
Depreciation			Total____		
Bad Debts			Other Additions (Describe)____		
Advertising			Total		
Interest			Less: Withdrawals or Dividends		
Taxes—Other Than Income			Other Deductions (Explain)		
Insurance			Total Deductions____		
Other Expenses			Net Worth or Capital Funds on This Financial Statement____		
Net Profit from Operations			**DETAIL OF INVENTORY**		
Other Income					
Less Other Expense			Is Inventory Figure Actual or Estimated?____		
Net Profit Before Income Tax			By Whom Taken or Estimated_____When?____		
Federal and State Income Tax			Buy Principally From____		
Net Profit or Loss			Average Terms of Purchase_____Sale____		
(To Net Worth or Earned Surplus)			Time of Year Inventory Maximum_____Minimum____		

FINANCIAL STATEMENT—FIRM OR CORPORATION—WOLCOTTS FORM 2001   (price class 6-2)

BUSINESS FINANCIAL HISTORY
(page 2)

SCHEDULE A — LIST OF REAL ESTATE AND IMPROVEMENTS WITH ENCUMBRANCES THEREON

DESCRIPTION, STREET NUMBER, LOCATION	TITLE IN NAMES OF	BOOK VALUE		MORTGAGES OR LIENS		TERMS OF PAYMENT	HOLDER OF LIEN
		LAND	IMPROVEMENTS	MATURITY	AMOUNT		
		$	$		$	$	
TOTALS		$	$		$	$	

SCHEDULE B — STOCKS & BONDS: Describe Fully. Use Supplemental Sheet if Necessary. Indicate if Stocks Are Common or Preferred. Give Interest Rate and Maturity of Bonds.

NO. OF SHARES AMT. OF BONDS	NAME AND ISSUE (DESCRIBE FULLY)	BOOK VALUE		MARKET VALUE	
		LISTED	UNLISTED	PRICE	VALUE
		$	$		$
	TOTALS	$	$		$

SCHEDULE C — Complete if Statement is for an Individual or Sole Proprietorship

Age _____ Number of Years in Present Business _____ Date of Filing Fictitious Trade Style _____

What Property Listed in This Statement is in Joint Tenancy? _____ Name of Other Party _____

What Property Listed in This Statement is Community Property? _____ Name of Other Party _____

With What Other Business Are You Connected? _____ Have You Filed Homestead? _____

Do You Deal With or Carry Accounts With Stockbrokers? _____ Amount $ _____ Name of Firm _____

SCHEDULE D — Complete if Statement is of a Partnership

NAME OF PARTNERS (INDICATE SPECIAL PARTNERS)	AGE	AMOUNT CONTRIBUTED	OUTSIDE NET WORTH	OTHER BUSINESS CONNECTIONS
		$	$	

Date of Organization _____ Limited or General? _____ Terminates _____

If Operating Under Fictitious Trade Style, Give Date of Filing _____

SCHEDULE E — Complete if Statement is of a Corporation

	AUTHORIZED	PAR VALUE	OUTSTANDING		ISSUED FOR	
			SHARES	AMOUNT	CASH	OTHER (DESCRIBE)
Common Stock	$	$		$	$	
Preferred Stock	$	$		$	$	

Bonds—Total Issue $ _____ Outstanding $ _____ Due _____ Interest Rate _____

Date Incorporated _____ Under Laws of State of _____

OFFICERS	AGE	SHARES OWNED		DIRECTORS AND PRINCIPAL STOCKHOLDERS	SHARES OWNED	
		COMMON	PREFERRED		COMMON	PREFERRED
President				Director		
Vice President				Director		
Secretary				Director		
Treasurer						

SCHEDULE F — Complete in ALL Cases   INSURANCE

Are Your Books Audited by Outside Accountants? Name _____	Merchandise _____ $ _____	Automobiles and Trucks:
Date of Last Audit _____ To What Date Has the U.S. Internal Revenue Department Examined Your Books? _____	Machinery & Fixtures _____ $ _____	Public Liability $ _____ M/$ _____ M
Are You Borrowing From Any Other Branch of This Bank? _____ Which? _____	Buildings _____ $ _____	Collision _____ $ _____
Are You Applying for Credit At Any Other Source? _____ Where? _____	Earthquake _____ $ _____	Property Damage _____ $ _____
Have You Ever Failed in Business? _____ If So, Attach a Complete Explanation and State Basis of Settlement With Creditors _____	Is Extended Coverage Endorsement Included? _____	Life Insurance _____ $ _____ Name of Beneficiary _____
Lease Has _____ Years to Run, With Monthly Rental of $ _____	Do You Carry Workmen's Compensation Insurance? _____	

STATEMENT OF BANK OFFICER:
Insofar as our records reveal, this Financial Statement is accurate and true. The foregoing statement is (a copy of) the original signed by the maker, in the credit files of this Bank.

_____
ASSISTANT CASHIER-MANAGER

The undersigned solemnly declares and certifies that the above statement (or in lieu thereof, the attached statement, as the case may be) and supporting schedules, both printed and written, give a full, true, and correct statement of the financial condition of the undersigned as of the date indicated.

Signature _____

By _____

(TITLE, IF CORPORATION)

LAST WORD ON FINANCIAL DOCUMENTS

The Financial Documents we have presented will most probably be sufficient for both your own use and that of potential lenders. Some of the documents may not be required. You should also note that we may have omitted forms required by some lenders. The important thing to note in the compiling of all financial statements is that the information must be correct, it must reflect the conclusions in the Organizational and Marketing Plans and you must have supportive records to back up your figures.

REMEMBER

The information in your Business Plan is not only to aid you in dealing with a lender. More important, it is for your own use on an ongoing basis. If you have done your homework, the financial documents you have prepared will be invaluable to you in the assessment of your operation and may very well be the determining factor in whether or not you achieve success in your business!

Supporting Documents

Now that you have completed the main body of your Business Plan, it is time to consider any additional records that pertain to your business and that should be included in your business plan.

Supporting Documents are the records that back up the statements and decisions made in the three main parts of your Business Plan. This chapter covers most of the documents that you will want to include. They will be discussed in the following order:

Personal Resumes

Owner's Financial Statement

Credit Reports

Copies of Leases

Letters of Reference

Contracts

Legal Documents

Location Studies, Demographics, etc.

Supporting Documents

After completing the main body of your Business Plan, you are now ready to consider the **Supporting Documents** that should be included. These are the records that back up the statements and decisions made in the three main parts of your Business Plan. As you are compiling the first three sections, it is a good idea to keep a separate list of the Supporting Documents that you mention or that come to mind. For instance, discussion of your business location might indicate a need for demographic studies, location maps, area studies, leases, etc. If you are considering applying for a loan to purchase equipment, your supporting documents might be existing equipment purchase agreements or lease contracts. By listing these items as you think of them, you will have a fairly complete list of all of your supporting documents by the time you reach this part of your task. You will be ready to sort them into a logical sequence and add any new ones that come to mind at this time.

Note: All supporting documents need not be included in every copy of your Business Plan. Include only that information you think will be needed by the potential lender. The rest should be kept with your copy of the plan and be easily accessible should it be requested by the lender. The following pages will cover most of the documents you will normally need to include:

PERSONAL RESUMES

If you are a sole proprietor, include your own resume. If your business is a partnership, there should be a resume for each partner. If you are a corporation, include resumes for all officers of the corporation. A resume need not and should not be a lengthy document. Preferably, it should be contained on one page for easy reading. Include the following categories and information:

- **Work History:** name of business with dates of employment. Begin with most recent. Include duties and responsibilities.

- **Educational Background:** schools and dates you attended, degrees earned, fields of concentration.

- **Professional Affiliations and Honors:** list organizations to which you belong that will add to your credibility. Tell about any awards that you or your business has received that sets you apart from others in your field.

- **Special Skills:** (for example: relates well to others, able to organize, not afraid to take risks, etc.)

If you find it difficult to write your own resume, there are professionals who will do it for you for a nominal fee. A well-written resume will be a useful tool and should always be kept up-to-date. Once written, it is a simple task to update your information, adding new items and eliminating those that will not benefit you in your current endeavors.

OWNER'S FINANCIAL STATEMENT

This is a statement of personal assets and liabilities. Information can be compiled in the same manner as a Balance Sheet. Use the same format and list all assets and liabilities to determine net worth. If you are a new business owner, your personal financial statement will be a part of the Financial Documents section and may be a standard form supplied by the potential lender.

CREDIT REPORTS

Credit ratings are of two types, business and personal. If you are already in business, you may have a Dun & Bradstreet rating. You can ask your suppliers or wholesalers to supply you with letters of credit. Personal credit ratings can be obtained through credit bureaus, banks and companies with whom you have dealt on a basis other than cash.

COPIES OF LEASES

Include all lease agreements currently in force between your company and a leasing agency. Some examples are the lease agreement for your business premises, equipment, automobiles, etc.

LETTERS OF REFERENCE

These are letters recommending you as being a reputable and reliable business person worthy of being considered a good risk. There are two types of letters of reference:

- **Business references:** written by business associates, suppliers and customers.
- **Personal References:** written by nonbusiness associates who can assess your business skills, not by friends or relatives. The new business owner will have to utilize personal references.

CONTRACTS

Include all business contracts, both completed and currently in force. Some examples are:

- **Current loan contracts**
- **Papers on prior business loans**
- **Purchase agreements on large equipment**
- **Vehicle purchase contracts**
- **Service contracts**
- **Maintenance agreements**
- **Miscellaneous contracts**

LEGAL DOCUMENTS

Include all legal documents pertaining to your business. Examples are:

- **Articles of incorporation**
- **Partnership agreement**
- **Copyrights, trademarks and patents**
- **Insurance policies, agreements, etc.**
- **Property and vehicle titles**

MISCELLANEOUS DOCUMENTS

These are all the documents (other than the above) which are referred to, but not included, in the Organizational and Marketing sections of your Business Plan. A good example of what we mean should be those records related to selecting your location in the Organizational or Marketing Plan. Your location might be finalized as the result of the development of a **Location Plan.** You can refer to this section in your Table of Contents. The potential lender can then turn to this portion of your plan and examine the Location Plan, which includes:

- **Demographic studies**
- **Map of selected location**
- **Area studies (crime rate, income, etc.)**

TO HELP YOU

The next three pages contain samples of a resume and a personal financial statement. If you have trouble creating your own resume, you might consider it worthwhile to have it done by a professional.

Sample Resume

JOHN SMITH
742 South Street
Jamestown, NY 10081
(207) 814-0221

WORK EXPERIENCE

1985 - Present   **ABC CORPORATION**
Burke, New York
Corporate President: Overall management responsibility for tool and die manufacture providing specialized parts to the aerospace industry. Specific management of Research and Development Department.

1980 - 1985   **ABC COMPONENTS**
Jamestown, New York
Sole Proprietor and General Manager: Sole responsibility for research and development of specialty aircraft parts. Long-term goal of expanding to incorporate and provide specialty parts to aerospace industry.

1970 - 1980   **JACKSON AIRCRAFT CO.**
Burke, New York
Quality Control Supervisor: Responsibility for the development and implementation of a quality control program for automated aircraft assembly facility.

EDUCATION

University of California, Berkeley - Master of Business Administration, emphasis on Marketing, 1980.
Stanford University, Palo Alto, CA - Bachelor of Civil Engineering, 1970.

PROFESSIONAL AFFILIATIONS

American Society of Professional Engineers
New York City Industrial League
Burke Chamber of Commerce

SPECIAL RECOGNITION

New York Businessman of the Year, 1992
New York Council on Small Business, 1992 - present
Director, Burke Chamber of Commerce

SPECIAL SKILLS

Resourceful and well-organized; Relate well to employees;
Self-motivated and not afraid to take risks.

PERSONAL
FINANCIAL HISTORY

PERSONAL FINANCIAL STATEMENT

(DO NOT USE FOR BUSINESS)

As of _____ _____ 19 _____

Received at _____ Branch

Name _____

Employed by _____ Years _____

Address _____

Position _____ Age _____ Name of Spouse _____

If Employed Less Than
1 Year, Previous Employer _____

The undersigned, for the purpose of procuring and establishing credit from time to time with you and to induce you to permit the undersigned to become indebted to you on notes, endorsements, guarantees, overdrafts or otherwise, furnishes the following (or in lieu thereof the attached) which is the most recent statement prepared by or for the undersigned as being a full, true and correct statement of the financial condition of the undersigned on the date indicated, and agrees to notify you immediately of the extent and character of any material change in said financial condition, and also agrees that if the undersigned, or any endorser or guarantor of any of the obligations of the undersigned, at any time fails in business or becomes insolvent, or commits an act of bankruptcy, or dies, or if a writ of attachment, garnishment, execution or other legal process be issued against property of the undersigned or if any assessment for taxes against the undersigned, other than taxes on real property, is made by the federal or state government or any department thereof, or if any of the representations made below prove to be untrue, or if the undersigned fails to notify you of any material change as above agreed, or if such change occurs, or if the business, or any interest therein, of the undersigned is sold, then and in such case, all of the obligations of the undersigned to you or held by you shall immediately be due and payable, without demand or notice. This statement shall be construed by you to be a continuing statement of the condition of the undersigned, and a new and original statement of all assets and liabilities upon each and every transaction in and by which the undersigned hereafter becomes indebted to you, until the undersigned advises in writing to the contrary.

ASSETS	DOLLARS	cents	LIABILITIES	DOLLARS	cents
Cash in B of _____ (Branch)			Notes payable B of _____ (Branch)		
Cash in _____ (Other - give name)			Notes payable _____ (Other)		
Accounts Receivable-Good _____			Accounts payable _____		
Stocks and Bonds (Schedule B) _____			Taxes payable _____		
Notes Receivable-Good _____			Contracts payable _____ (To whom)		
Cash Surrender Value Life Insurance _____			Contracts payable _____ (To whom)		
Autos _____ (Year-Make) _____ (Year—Make)			Real Estate indebtedness (Schedule A) _____		
Real Estate (Schedule A) _____			Other Liabilities (describe)		
Other Assets (describe)			1. _____		
1. _____			2. _____		
2. _____			3. _____		
3. _____			4. _____		
4. _____			TOTAL LIABILITIES NET WORTH		
5. _____					
TOTAL ASSETS			TOTAL		

ANNUAL INCOME			and ANNUAL EXPENDITURES (Excluding Ordinary living expenses)		
Salary _____			Real Estate payment (s) _____		
Salary (wife or husband) _____			Rent _____		
Securities Income _____			Income Taxes _____		
Rentals _____			Insurance Premiums _____		
Other (describe)			Property Taxes _____		
1. _____			Other (describe-include instalment payments other than real estate)		
2. _____			1. _____		
3. _____			2. _____		
4. _____			3. _____		
5. _____					
TOTAL INCOME			TOTAL EXPENDITURES		

LESS-TOTAL EXPENDITURES

NET CASH INCOME
(exclusive of ordinary living expenses) _____

PERSONAL
FINANCIAL HISTORY
(page 2)

What assets in this statement are in joint tenancy? _____ Name of other Party _____

Have you filed homestead? _____

Are you a guarantor on anyone's debt? _____ If so, give details _____

Are any encumbered assets or debts secured except as indicated? _____ If so, please itemize by debt and security _____

_____

Do you have any other business connections? _____ If so, give details _____

Are there any suits or judgments against you? _____ Any pending? _____

Have you gone through bankruptcy or compromised a debt? _____

Have you made a will? _____ Number of dependents _____

SCHEDULE A—REAL ESTATE

Location and type of Improvement	Title in Name of	Estimated Value	Amount Owing	To Whom Payable
		$	$	

SCHEDULE B—STOCKS AND BONDS

Number of Shares Amount of Bonds	Description	Current Market on Listed	Estimated Value on Unlisted
		$	$

If additional space is needed for Schedule A and/or Schedule B, list on separate sheet and attach.

INSURANCE

Life Insurance $ _____ Name of Company _____ Beneficiary _____

Automobile Insurance:
Public Liability — yes ☐   no ☐   Property Damage — yes ☐   no ☐
Comprehensive personal Liability—yes ☐   no ☐

STATEMENT OF BANK OFFICER:	
Insofar as our records reveal, this Financial Statement is accurate and true. The foregoing statement is (a copy of) the original signed by the maker, in the credit files of this bank.	The undersigned certifies that the above statement (or in lieu thereof, the attached statement, as the case may be) and supporting schedules, both printed and written, give a full, true, and correct statement of the financial condition of the undersigned as of the date indicated.
_____ Assistant Cashier Manager	Date signed Signature

CHAPTER VIII

Tax Information: An Important Aid to Writing Your Business Plan

A basic understanding of the U.S. tax system is an absolute necessity if you are going to write a Business Plan. It has long been a premise of the majority of taxpayers that the system is unwieldy, complicated, unfair and a plague to most Americans. If you will overlook that discontent for a moment, we will attempt to show you how a basic understanding of the tax system can be an invaluable aid to you during business planning.

We have also included some visual aids and lists that should help you with your business planning in relation to taxes.

Calendars of Federal Taxes

Free IRS Publications

Information Resources

Tax Information

COMPARING OUR TAX SYSTEM AND SMALL BUSINESS ACCOUNTING

Looking at the tax system and small business accounting is like studying the chicken and the egg. They cannot be separated. Many new business owners attempt to set up a recordkeeping system without examining and understanding the Internal Revenue Service's tax forms to be completed at the end of the year. This is a gross error for two reasons. The first is failure to account for financial information required by the IRS at tax time. More important, however, is the failure to utilize information and services that will help you to develop an effective recordkeeping system, which will, in turn, enable you to analyze your business and implement changes to keep it on the track to profitability.

In order that you can better comprehend the relationship between business planning and the tax system, we will introduce you to two tax forms and show you how you can benefit from understanding those forms.

SCHEDULE C (FORM 1040)

This form is entitled "Profit or (Loss) From Business or Profession" (required tax reporting form for all sole proprietors).

a. **Information required:** Gross receipts or sales, beginning and ending inventories, labor, materials, goods purchased, returns and allowances, deductions, and net profit or loss. The net profit is the figure upon which your income tax liability is based.

b. **Benefits of understanding:** In order to provide the year-end information required on a Schedule C and to figure income tax liability, it will be necessary for you to set up a recordkeeping system that includes a general ledger, petty cash record, payroll records, inventory records, a fixed asset log (depreciation record), accounts payable and accounts receivable. An examination of the entries on a Schedule C will help you to determine the fixed and variable expense categories to be used in your general ledger. It will also tell you how to sort out petty cash expenses so they may be categorized by type of expense. In addition to the setting up of categories for keeping expenses in a general ledger, you will want to divide types of income as well. This will tell you which sources are the most profitable for your business. Year-end totals of income and expense items are used to develop profit & loss statements. Fixed asset records, inventory records, accounts receivable, accounts payable, etc. are used to develop balance sheets. These are the two most important of the financial statements used to analyze your business.

Note: Form 1065, "U.S. Partnership Return of Income" and Form 1120-A or Form 1120, "U.S. Corporation Income Tax Returns" are used for these legal structures.

SCHEDULE SE (FORM 1040)

This form is entitled "Computation of Social Security Self-Employment Tax."

a. **Information required:** Computation of the business owner's contribution to Social Security. As the business owner, you are now the employer and the employee. This tax is paid as a part of your estimated tax (1040ES) each quarter.

b. **Benefits of understanding:** Schedule SE will help you to compute your tax liability, which can be translated into your Cash Flow Statement. Failure to familiarize yourself with the requirements on how to compute this tax and know what percentage of your net income will be owed will result in a false picture as to the net profit of your business. Don't forget—the IRS is interested in your net profit **before** taxes. You are concerned with net profit **after** taxes.

FEDERAL TAXES FOR WHICH YOU MAY BE LIABLE

Familiarize yourself with the federal taxes for which you may be liable and the times at which they will have to be paid. Your cash flow statement will have to reflect these payments. If you fail to include taxes to be paid, you will find yourself with an unbalanced budget and a serious cash deficiency could result.

The tax calendars we have developed and provided in this chapter should be of some help to you in this aspect. We have set them up according to the date of the liability. Paste a copy of the one pertaining to your legal structure on the wall as a visual reminder. Be sure to look ahead as the due dates are firm and a penalty may be imposed for not reporting on time.

CALENDARS OF FEDERAL TAXES

As you can see from the above examples, examination of required tax forms and the understanding of allowable business deductions can lead to the discovery of many types of records that you will need and profit from in your business. That same examination will also lead a smart business owner with an inquiring mind to a thousand questions left unanswered.

1. How do I set up my records?

2. What accounting method is required for my business?

3. How do I determine what is and what is not deductible?

4. Is inventory based on cost or sale price?

5. What is an independent contractor?

6. What are the rules pertaining to home-based businesses?

7. What items are depreciable—and at what rate?

8. How are automobile expenses figured?

9. As a business owner, can I invest in tax-deferred savings?

10. What is an S corporation?

11. What is the basis for determination of the tax year?

12. What travel expenses are allowable?

13. Is it better to lease or purchase a vehicle?

14. When do I start paying estimated taxes?

15. What is the best legal structure for my business?

What most of us don't know is that the United States government has spent a great deal of time and money to make free publications available for preparation of income taxes. Those same publications will answer all of your questions and some that have not yet occurred to you. They will also provide you with many samples of business statements and information on how to complete them.

Make It Your Business

To Send For And Study These Publications!!

We have many students with great ideas for a product or service, but no desire to concern themselves with paperwork and recordkeeping. Those businesses are doomed to failure. We cannot place too much emphasis on the importance of understanding your business recordkeeping and its inter-relationship with tax accounting. Financial analysis will help to make your profits grow.

It is important that you set up a tax information file and also that you keep it current. Make it your business to update your file with new publications. Study the revisions that take place in our tax laws. Remember that your Business Plan is an ongoing process requiring the implementation of many changes. You may rest assured that many of those changes will be a direct result of new tax laws.

TO HELP YOU UNDERSTAND TAXES AND SET UP A FILE OF IRS PUBLICATIONS

In order to aid you in your business, we have devoted the remainder of this chapter to providing you with the following:

1. **Calendars of federal taxes** for which a sole proprietor, partnership, S corporation or corporation may be liable. You will find four calendars. Choose the one that is appropriate to your legal structure.

2. **A list of free publications** available from the IRS that will be helpful to business owners. We strongly suggest that you send for all of them on a yearly basis. Keep them in a three-ring binder so that you can refer to them as the need arises. These publications are updated every November and can be ordered shortly thereafter.

3. **An information page** telling you where and how to send for free forms and publications. You can request them by mail or simply call a toll free number and ask for them by number.

SOLE PROPRIETOR
Calendar of Federal Taxes for Which You May Be Liable

Month	Day	Description	Form
January	15	Estimated tax	Form 1040ES
	31	Social security (FICA) tax and the withholding of income tax Note: See IRS rulings for deposit - Pub. 334	941, 941E, 942 & 943
	31	Providing information on social security (FICA) tax and the withholding of income tax	W-2 (to employee)
	31	Federal unemployment (FUTA) tax	940-EZ or 940
	31	Federal unemployment (FUTA) tax (only if liability for unpaid taxes exceeds $100)	8109 (to make deposits)
	31	Information returns to nonemployees and transactions with other persons	Form 1099 (to recipients)
February	28	Information returns to nonemployees and transactions with other persons	Form 1099 (to IRS)
	28	Providing information on social security (FICA) tax and the withholding income tax	W-2 & W-3 (to Soc. Sec. Admin.)
April	15	Income tax	Schedule C (Form 1040)
	15	Self-employment tax	Schedule SE (Form 1040)
	15	Estimated tax	Form 1040ES
	30	Social security (FICA) tax and the withholding of income tax Note: See IRS rulings for deposit - Pub. 334	941, 941E 942 & 943
	30	Federal unemployment (FUTA) tax (only if liability for unpaid taxes exceeds $100)	8109 (to make deposits)
June	15	Estimated tax	Form 1040ES
July	31	Social security (FICA) tax and the withholding of income tax Note: See IRS rulings for deposit - Pub. 334	941, 941E, 942 & 943
	31	Federal unemployment (FUTA) tax (only if liability for unpaid taxes exceeds $100)	8109 (to make deposits)
September	15	Estimated tax	Form 1040ES
October	31	Social security (FICA) tax and the withholding of income tax Note: See IRS rulings for deposit - Pub. 334	941, 941E, 941 & 943
	31	Federal unemployment (FUTA) tax (only if liability for unpaid taxes exceeds $100)	8109 (to make deposits)

If your tax year is not January 1st through December 31st:

- Schedule C (Form 1040) is due the 15th day of the 4th month after end of the tax year. Schedule SE is due same day as Form 1040.
- Estimated tax (1040ES) is due the 15th day of 4th, 6th, and 9th months of tax year, and the 15th day of 1st month after the end of tax year.

PARTNERSHIP
Calendar of Federal Taxes for Which You May Be Liable

January	15	Estimated tax (individual who is a partner)	Form 1040ES
	31	Social security (FICA) tax and the withholding of income tax Note: See IRS rulings for deposit - Pub. 334	941, 941E, 942 & 943
	31	Providing information on soc. security (FICA) tax and the withholding of income tax	W-2 (to employee)
	31	Federal unemployment (FUTA) tax	940-EZ or 940
	31	Federal unemployment (FUTA) tax (only if liability for unpaid taxes exceeds $100)	8109 (to make deposits)
	31	Information returns to nonemployees and transactions with other persons	Form 1099 (to recipients)
February	28	Information returns to nonemployees and transactions with other persons	Form 1099 (to IRS)
	28	Providing information on social security (FICA) tax and on withholding income tax	W-2 & W-3 (to Soc. Sec. Admin.)
April	15	Income tax (individual who is a partner)	Schedule C (Form 1040)
	15	Annual return of income	Form 1065
	15	Self-employment tax (individual who is partner)	Schedule SE (Form 1040)
	15	Estimated tax (individual who is partner)	Form 1040ES
	30	Social security (FICA) tax and the withholding of income tax Note: See IRS rulings for deposit - Pub. 334	941, 941E 942 & 943
	30	Federal unemployment (FUTA) tax (only if liability for unpaid taxes exceeds $100)	8109 (to make deposits)
June	15	Estimated tax (individual who is a partner)	Form 1040ES
July	31	Social security (FICA) tax and the withholding of income tax Note: See IRS rulings for deposit - Pub. 334	941, 941E, 942 & 943
	31	Federal unemployment (FUTA) tax (only if liability for unpaid taxes exceeds $100)	8109 (to make deposits)
September	15	Estimated tax (individual who is a partner)	Form 1040ES
October	31	Social security (FICA) tax and the withholding of income tax Note: See IRS rulings for deposit - Pub. 334	941, 941E, 941 & 943
	31	Federal unemployment (FUTA) tax (only if liability for unpaid taxes exceeds $100)	8109 (to make deposits)

If your Tax Year is not January 1st through December 31st:
- Income tax is due the 15th day of the 4th month after end of tax year.
- Self-employment tax is due the same day as income tax (Form 1040).
- Estimated tax (1040ES) is due the 15th day of the 4th, 6th, and 9th month of the tax year and the 15th day of 1st month after end of the tax year.

S CORPORATION
Calendar of Federal Taxes for Which You May Be Liable

January	15	Estimated tax (individual S corp. shareholder)	Form 1040ES
	31	Social security (FICA) tax and the withholding of income tax Note: See IRS rulings for deposit - Pub. 334	941, 941E, 942 & 943
	31	Providing information on social security (FICA) tax and the withholding of income tax	W-2 (to employee)
	31	Federal unemployment (FUTA) tax	940-EZ or 940
	31	Federal unemployment (FUTA) tax (only if liability for unpaid taxes exceeds $100)	8109 (to make deposits)
	31	Information returns to nonemployees and transactions with other persons	Form 1099 (to recipients)
February	28	Information returns to nonemployees and transactions with other persons	Form 1099 (to IRS)
	28	Providing information on social security (FICA) tax and the withholding of income tax	W-2 & W-3 (to Soc. Sec. Admin.)
March	15	Income tax	1120S
April	15	Income tax (individual S corp. shareholder)	Form 1040
	15	Estimated tax (individual S corp. shareholder)	Form 1040ES
	30	Social security (FICA) tax and the withholding of income tax Note: See IRS rulings for deposit - Pub. 334	941, 941E 942 & 943
	30	Federal unemployment (FUTA) tax (only if liability for unpaid taxes exceeds $100)	8109 (to make deposits)
June	15	Estimated tax (individual S corp. shareholder)	Form 1040ES
July	31	Social security (FICA) tax and the withholding of income tax Note: See IRS rulings for deposit - Pub. 334	941, 941E, 942 & 943
	31	Federal unemployment (FUTA) tax (only if liability for unpaid taxes exceeds $100)	8109 (to make deposits)
September	15	Estimated tax (individual S corp. shareholder)	Form 1040ES
October	31	Social security (FICA) tax and the withholding of income tax Note: See IRS rulings for deposit - Pub. 334	941, 941E, 941 & 943
	31	Federal unemployment (FUTA) tax (only if liability for unpaid taxes exceeds $100)	8109 (to make deposits)

If your tax year is not January 1st through December 31st:

- S corp. income tax (1120S) and individual S corp shareholder income tax (Form 1040) are due the 15th day of the 4th month after end of tax year.

- Estimated tax of indiv. shareholder (1040ES) is due 15th day of 4th, 6th, and 9th months of tax year and 15th day of 1st month after end of tax year.

CORPORATION
Calendar of Federal Taxes for Which You May Be Liable

Month	Day	Description	Form
January	31	Social security (FICA) tax and the withholding of income tax Note: See IRS rulings for deposit - Pub. 334	941, 941E, 942 & 943
	31	Providing information on social security (FICA) tax and the withholding of income tax	W-2 (to employee)
	31	Federal unemployment (FUTA) tax	940-EZ or 940
	31	Federal unemployment (FUTA) tax (only if liability for unpaid taxes exceeds $100)	8109 (to make deposits)
	31	Information returns to nonemployees and transactions with other persons	Form 1099 (to recipients)
February	28	Information returns to nonemployees and transactions with other persons	Form 1099 (to IRS)
	28	Providing information on social security (FICA) tax and the withholding of income tax	W-2 & W-3 (to Soc. Sec. Admin.)
March	15	Income tax	1120 or 1120-A
April	15	Estimated tax	1120-W
	30	Social security (FICA) tax and the withholding of income tax Note: See IRS rulings for deposit - Pub. 334	941, 941E 942 & 943
	30	Federal unemployment (FUTA) tax (only if liability for unpaid taxes exceeds $100)	8109 (to make deposits)
June	15	Estimated tax	1120-W
July	31	Social security (FICA) tax and the withholding of income tax Note: See IRS rulings for deposit - Pub. 334	941, 941E, 942 & 943
	31	Federal unemployment (FUTA) tax (only if liability for unpaid taxes exceeds $100)	8109 (to make deposits)
September	15	Estimated tax	1120-W
October	31	Social security (FICA) tax and the withholding of income tax Note: See IRS rulings for deposit - Pub. 334	941, 941E, 941 & 943
	31	Federal unemployment (FUTA) tax (only if liability for unpaid taxes exceeds $100)	8109 (to make deposits)
December	15	Estimated tax	1120-W

If your tax year is not January 1st through December 31st:

- Income tax (Form 1120 or 1120-A) is due on the 15th day of the 3rd month after the end of the tax year.
- Estimated tax (1120-W) is due the 5th day of the 4th, 6th, 9th, and 12th months of the tax year.

FREE PUBLICATIONS AVAILABLE FROM THE IRS

The following is a list of the publications referred to in the preceding material, along with others that may prove helpful to you in the course of your business. Make it a point to keep a file of tax information. Send for these publications and update your file with new publications at least once a year. The United States government has spent a great deal of time and money to make this information available to you for preparation of income tax returns.

Information on ordering these publications can be found following this listing. Or if you prefer, you may call IRS toll free at 1-800-TAX-FORM (1-800-829-3676).

For a complete listing: Publication 910, *Guide to Free Tax Services*

Begin by reading the two following publications. They will give you the most comprehensive information.

334 - *Tax Guide for Small Business*

910 - *Guide to Free Tax Services*

These publications are good to have on hand as reference material and will answer most questions you have relating to specific topics:

15 - *Circular E., Employer's Tax Guide*

17 - *Your Federal Income Tax*

463 - *Travel, Entertainment and Gift Expenses*

505 - *Tax Withholding and Estimated Tax*

508 - *Educational Expenses*

509 - *Tax Calendars for Current Year*

510 - *Excise Taxes for Current Year*

533 - *Self-Employment Tax*

534 - *Depreciation*

IRS PUBLICATION LIST - cont.

535 - *Business Expenses*

536 - *Net Operating Losses*

538 - *Accounting Periods & Methods*

541 - *Tax Information on Partnerships*

542 - *Tax Information on Corporations*

547 - *Nonbusiness Disasters, Casualties, Theft*

551 - *Basis of Assets*

557 - *Tax-Exempt Status for Your Organization*

560 - *Retirement Plans for the Self-Employed*

583 - *Taxpayers Starting a Business*

587 - *Business Use of Your Home*

589 - *Tax Information on S Corporations*

594 - *The Collection Process (Employment Tax Accounts)*

596 - *Earned Income Credit*

908 - *Bankruptcy and Other Debt Cancellation*

911 - *Tax Information for Direct Sellers*

917 - *Business Use of a Car*

925 - *Passive Activity & At Risk Rules*

937 - *Business Reporting*

946 - *How to Begin Depreciating Your Property*

947 - *Power of Attorney and Practice Before the IRS*

1544 - *Reporting Cash Payments of Over $10,000 (Received in a Trade or Business)*

Order Information
for
IRS Forms and Publications

Resource:
IRS Pub. 910
(Rev. 11-91)

Where to Send Your Order for Free Forms and Publications

Save Time

Participating libraries have IRS tax forms available for copying and reference sets of Tax Information Publications. Also, participating banks, post offices, and libraries stock Forms 1040, 1040A, 1040EZ, their instructions, Schedules A&B, and EIC, and Schedules 1 and 2.

If you live in:	Send to:	For other locations, see below:
Alaska, Arizona, California, Colorado, Hawaii, Idaho, Montana, Nevada, New Mexico, Oregon, Utah, Washington, Wyoming	Western Area Distribution Center Rancho Cordova, CA 95743-0001	**Foreign Addresses—** Taxpayers with mailing addresses in foreign countries should send this order blank to either: Eastern Area Distribution Center, P.O. Box 85074, Richmond, VA 23261-5074; or Western Area Distribution Center, Rancho Cordova, CA 95743-0001, whichever is closer. Send letter requests for other forms and publications to: Eastern Area Distribution Center, P.O. Box 85074, Richmond, VA 23261-5074.
Alabama, Arkansas, Illinois, Indiana, Iowa, Kansas, Kentucky, Louisiana, Michigan, Minnesota, Mississippi, Missouri, Nebraska, North Dakota, Ohio, Oklahoma, South Dakota, Tennessee, Texas, Wisconsin	Central Area Distribution Center P.O. Box 9903 Bloomington, IL 61799	
Connecticut, Delaware, District of Columbia, Florida, Georgia, Maine, Maryland, Massachusetts, New Hampshire, New Jersey, New York, North Carolina, Pennsylvania, Rhode Island, South Carolina, Vermont, Virginia, West Virginia	Eastern Area Distribution Center P.O. Box 85074 Richmond, VA 23261-5074	**Puerto Rico—**Eastern Area Distribution Center, P.O. Box 85074, Richmond, VA 23261-5074. **Virgin Islands—**V.I. Bureau of Internal Revenue, Lockharts Garden No. 1A, Charlotte Amalie, St. Thomas, VI 00802

Distribution Centers

Detach at this Line

Circle Desired Forms, Instructions, and Publications

We will send you two copies of each form and one copy of each publication or set of instructions you circle. Please cut the order blank on the dotted line and **be sure to print or type your name and address accurately on the other side.**

To help reduce waste, please order only the items you think you will need to prepare your return. Use the blank spaces to order items not listed. If you need more space, attach a separate sheet of paper listing the additional items you need.

Order Blank

1040	Schedule F (1040)	Schedule 3 (1040A) & instructions	2210 & instructions	8582 & instructions	Pub. 508	Pub. 590
Instructions for 1040 & Schedules	Schedule R (1040) & instructions	1040EZ	2441 & instructions	8822	Pub. 521	Pub. 596
Schedules A&B (1040)	Schedule SE (1040)	Instructions for 1040EZ	3903 & instructions	Pub. 1	Pub. 523	Pub. 910
Schedule C (1040)	1040A	1040-ES (1992)	4562 & instructions	Pub. 17	Pub. 525	Pub. 917
Schedule D (1040)	Instructions for 1040A & Schedules	1040X & instructions	4868	Pub. 334	Pub. 527	Pub. 929
Schedule E (1040)	Schedule 1 (1040A)	2106 & instructions	8283 & instructions	Pub. 463	Pub. 529	
Schedule EIC (1040A or 1040)	Schedule 2 (1040A)	2119 & instructions	8332	Pub. 505	Pub. 553	

Detach at this Line

Print or type your name and address on this label. It will be used to speed your order for forms to you.

Name

Number, Street, and Apartment Number

City, Town or Post Office, State and ZIP Code

Keeping Your Business Plan Up-To-Date

Your business plan will serve you well if you will revise it often and let it serve as your guide during the lifetime of your business. In order to update it, you as the owner will have the final responsibility to analyze what is happening and implement the changes that will make your business more profitable.

Changes Within the Company

Changes in Customer Needs

Changes in Technology

Keeping Your Business Plan Up-To-Date

REVISING YOUR BUSINESS PLAN

Revision is an ongoing process. Changes are constantly taking place in your business. If your Business Plan is going to be effective either to the business or to a potential lender, it will be necessary for you to update it on a regular basis. Changes necessitating such revisions can be attributed to three sources.

Changes Within the Company

You may be increasing or decreasing the number of employees, upgrading the skill level, adding new services or there may be any number of changes in your organization. You might decide to incorporate or add new partners. Be sure to document these changes.

Changes Originating with the Customer

Your product or service may show surges or declines due to your customers' changes in need or taste. This is evident in all the companies who fold because they continue to offer what they like instead of what the customer will buy or use. Polyester materials were popular for many years. Now the average buyer considers polyester as an inferior material. Clothing retailers are currently selling cotton, rayon and silk.

Changes in Technology

You will have to change your business to stay current with a changing world. As technology improves and there are new products on the market, you will have to keep up or you will be left behind. When quartz clocks and watches became commonplace, the service-man or dealer who stubbornly refused to add this technology to his or her business doomed the operation to decreased profits and probable failure.

IMPLEMENTING CHANGES IN YOUR BUSINESS PLAN

You, as the owner, must be aware of the changes in your industry, your market, and your community. First you must **determine what revisions are needed.** In order to make this determination, you will have to compare your business plan with the three types of changes discussed in the above paragraphs.

If this is an overwhelming task for one person, utilize your employees to keep track of the business trends applicable to their expertise. For example, your buyer can analyze the buying patterns of your customers and report to you.

Your research and development person might look at changes in technology and materials. Each department can be responsible for information that pertains to its particular area and report on a periodic basis.

Be aware, however, that the **final judgment as to revisions will rest with you, the owner.** You will have to analyze the information and decide on any changes to be implemented. If your decision is wrong, don't dwell on it. Correct your error and cut your losses as soon as possible. With experience, your percentage of correct decisions will increase and your reward will be higher profits.

ANTICIPATING YOUR PROBLEMS

Try to see ahead and determine what possible problems may arise to plague you. For example, you may have to deal with costs that exceed your projections. At the same time, you may experience a sharp decline in sales. These two factors occurring simultaneously can portend disaster if you are not ready for them.

Also, we might add, a good year can give you a false sense of security. Be cautious when things are too good. The increased profits may be temporary. As an example, antique clocks were selling extremely well and commanded high prices in the early 1980s. Those prices have decreased by about 40% today—and new clocks far outsell the antique ones.

You might think about developing an alternate budget based on possible problems. This also may be the time when you decide that emphasis on a service would be more profitable due to changes in the economy. To again use the clock business as an example, the repair business is currently going strong, even though retail trade is down.

DON'T FALL INTO THE TRAP!

More often than not, a business owner will spend a lot of time and effort writing a business plan when the pressure is on to borrow funds or to get a business started. The intention is there to always keep that plan up-to-date. Before long, things get hectic and the business plan is put in a drawer, never again to be seen.

There is an old saying that "the business that operates by the seat of it's pants will end up with torn pants."

DO REMEMBER TO REVISE YOUR PLAN OFTEN

Awareness of change in industry and revision according to those changes will benefit you greatly. Your business plan can be your best friend. If you nurture your relationship with it, you will have a running start on the path to success!

Putting Your Business Plan Together

If you have followed the steps presented in the preceding chapters of this book and gathered the materials and documents needed as supporting information, you are now ready to assemble your finished Business Plan.

In this chapter we will discuss the pros and cons of using business plan software. We will also give you some ideas on how to best put your plan together to help ensure that it will be more acceptable in the eyes and mind of the reader.

Business Planning Software

The Finished Product

The Last Word

Putting Your Business Plan Together

BUSINESS PLAN SOFTWARE

There are several software programs on the market today. What the prospective business plan writer hopes for is a quick solution to a difficult problem— a program with questions that can be answered by filling in the blanks after which the software will automatically generate a finished business plan.

Do Not Use A Canned Program. There are in fact some "fill in the blanks" software packages. However, we would not advise you to use this type of program. There are at least two good reasons for this:

1. Your business plan serves as the guide for your particular business. Even though you may have the same type of business as someone else, you will have different areas of focus and you will want to fill your own special niche by doing things that will be unique to your business. These differences should be reflected in your business plan. Therefore, a canned business plan cannot possibly serve you well.

2. If you are going to potential lenders or investors, you will find that they will readily recognize the canned statements from certain programs. This is an immediate indicator to that person that you have not put much time or effort into the planning process and that you may not know your business well enough to succeed at it. Since the repayment of your loan depends on your business skills, you may look like a poor risk.

Effective software programs should allow you to do your own research and generate your own organizational and marketing statements. This is the only way that you can create a plan that will make your business unique. The statements will show that you have researched your business and put some thought into how to run it effectively.

Automated financial statements (or spreadsheets) can be a great help to you in the Financial Section of your business plan. If they are pre-formatted and pre-formulated, you will save a great deal of time. You plug in the amounts to the allocated cells and the program should do all of your adding and subtracting. Since the Pro Forma Cash Flow statement has approximately 350 figures to work with, your time will be cut considerably. It will also allow you to make changes or create "what if" situations and see the results immediately.

Even here, a note of caution is called for. Preformatted spreadsheets will need to be altered to reflect the categories of revenues and expenses pertinent to your particular business. Be sure the program allows for these changes.

**Yes! We do have business planning software
that accounts for all of the above!**

In order to further implement the writing of your business plan, we have developed a software program called **"Automate Your Business Plan."** It is for IBM and compatibles, requires 640K of internal memory and **does not** require any additional software. It has its own full-powered word processor and an easy-to-use spreadsheet program with preformatted and preformulated financial statements that can be modified to match your business.

"Automate Your Business Plan" is *Anatomy of a Business Plan* translated into software. It follows the book step-by-step and will print out a finished business plan.

THE FINISHED PRODUCT

When you have finished writing your business plan, there are a few last considerations that will help in making a favorable impression with a potential lender or investor.

Binding and Cover

For your working business plan, it is best to use a three-ring binder. That way information can be easily added, updated or replaced. Your working plan should have a copy of all of your supporting documents. For the plan that you take to a potential lender or investor, you will want to bind it in a nice cover. You can purchase one from your local stationery store or take it to your printer and have it done. Use blue, brown or black covers. Bankers are usually conservative.

Length

Be concise! Generally, you should have no more than 30 to 40 pages in the plan you take to a lender, including your **Supporting Documents**. As you write each section, think of it as being a summary. Include as much information as you can in a brief statement. Potential lenders do not want to search through volumes of material to get to needed information.

Presentation

Do your best to make your plan look presentable. However, do not go to the unnecessary expense of paying for typesetting and high-powered computer graphics. This might be considered as frivolous by some lenders—a first impression that might indicate that you would not use their loan funds wisely.

Table of Contents

Be sure to include a Table of Contents in your Business Plan. It will follow the Statement of Purpose. Make it detailed enough so the lender can locate any of the areas addressed in the plan. It must also list the Supporting Documents and their corresponding page numbers. You may use the Table of Contents in this book (starting with "Statement of Purpose" and ending with "Supporting Documents") as a guide to compiling your own.

Number of Copies

Make copies for yourself and each lender you wish to approach. Keep track of each copy. Do not try to work with too many potential lenders at one time. If your loan is refused, be sure to retrieve your business plan.

THE LAST WORD

When you are finished, your Business Plan will look professional, but the lender should know that it was done by you. It will be the best indication a lender will have to judge your potential for success.

> *Be Sure That Your Business Plan Is*
> *Representative Of Your Best Efforts!!!*

It is our hope that you have been able to use this book to help you develop a concise, logical and appropriate plan for your business. When your work is done and your business plan is complete, don't forget to:

1. **Operate within your business plan.**
2. **Anticipate changes.**
3. **Revise your business plan and keep it up-to-date.**

Do these things and we will guarantee that you will be well on your way to improving your chances of success and growth as you continue with your business venture. Thank you for including our materials as part of your plan.

CHAPTER

XI

Information Resources

The information you need to research and run your business effectively can be found through the resources of public, corporate or university libraries, in governmental agencies and in civic organizations. One of our under-utilized resources is the public library. The reference librarian in the business section can direct you to the materials you need.

Take some time to write out your questions. Getting the answers will involve reading books, newsletters and periodicals on the subject of your business. You will contact trade and professional associations to get information on trade shows, industry trends and sources of supply. Attendance and participation at meetings of civic organizations such as chambers of commerce and at professional organizations unique to your business will provide opportunities for networking. Governmental departments issue publications containing statistical data and projections for their areas of concern. The Internal Revenue Service, Department of Commerce and the Small Business Administration offer low-cost classes concerning business development. Many colleges and community service programs now offer classes and seminars on business issues. The following reference section will help you locate resources that can provide the answers to your questions.

Library Resources

Indexes to Periodicals and Magazine Articles

U.S. Government Departments

Software, Books and Publications

Organizations and Associations

Information Resources

LIBRARY RESOURCES

Bacon's Newspaper/Magazine Directory (Bacon's Information): Lists media as source of publicity information.

Encyclopedia of Associations (Gale Research Company): Lists trade and professional associations throughout the United States, many of which publish newsletters and provide marketing information. These associations can help business owners keep up with the latest industry developments.

Encyclopedia of Business Information Sources (Gale Research Company): Lists handbooks, periodicals, directories, trade associations and more for 1200 plus specific industries and business subjects. Start here to search for information on your particular business.

U.S. Industrial Outlook (U.S. Department of Commerce): Provides an overview, forecasts and short profiles for 200 American industries, including statistics on recent trends and a five-year outlook.

Reference Book for World Traders (Alfred Croner): This three-volume set lists banks, chambers of commerce, customs, marketing organizations, invoicing procedures and more for 185 foreign markets. Sections on export planning, financing, shipping, laws and tariffs are also included, with a directory of helpful government agencies.

Incubators for Small Business (U.S. Small Business Administration): Lists more than 170 state government offices and incubators that offer financial and technical aid to new small businesses.

Small Business Sourcebook (Gale Research Company): A good starting place for finding consultants, educational institutions, governmental agencies offering assistance, as well as specific information sources for more than 140 types of businesses.

Sourcebook for Franchise Opportunities (Dow Jones-Irwin): Provides annual directory information for U.S. franchises, and data for investment requirements, royalty and advertising fees, services furnished by the franchiser, projected growth rates and locations where franchises are licensed to operate.

National Trade and Professional Associations of the U.S. (Columbia Books, Inc.): Indexes trade and professional associations by association, geographic region, subject and budget.

City and County Data Book (U.S. Department of Commerce): Updated every three years, contains statistical information on population, education, employment, income, housing and retail sales.

Standard Industrial Classification Manual (U.S. Department of Commerce): Lists the SIC numbers issued to major areas of business; for example, the SIC number for piano tuning is #7699. This unique number is used in locating statistical data.

Directory of Directories (Gale Research Company): Describes more than 9,000 buyer's guides and directories.

Dun and Bradstreet Million Dollar Directory (Dun and Bradstreet): Lists companies alphabetically, geographically and by product classification.

Statistical Abstract of the U.S. (U.S. Department of Commerce): Updated annually, provides demographic, economic and social information.

INDEXES TO PERIODICALS AND MAGAZINE ARTICLES

These references can be found in the library. Periodicals and articles can be researched by subject. Become familiar with periodicals and read articles that contain information specific to your type of business.

Business Periodicals Index (H.W. Wilson Company): Indexes articles published in 300 business-oriented periodicals.

Gale Directory of Publications (Gale Research Company): Lists periodicals and newsletters.

Magazines for Libraries (R.R. Bowker Company): Provides directory of publications.

New York Times Index (New York Times Company): Indexes articles published in the New York Times.

Reader's Guide to Periodical Literature (H.W. Wilson Company): Provides index to articles published in 200 popular magazines.

Ulrich's International Periodicals Directory (R.R. Bowker Company): Lists more than 100,000 magazines, newsletters, newspapers, journals and other periodicals in 554 subject areas.

U.S. GOVERNMENT DEPARTMENTS

Federal agencies offer resources that will help you research your industry. Also gather information from governmental agencies on your state and local level. The phone numbers listed are for a central office. You can be directed to the department that can meet your specific needs. Ask to be put on a mailing list for appropriate materials. Most departments issue a catalog for their publications.

Bureau of Consumer Protection
Division of Special Statutes
6th and Pennsylvania Avenue NW
Washington, DC 20580

Consumer Information Center
P.O. Box 100
Pueblo, CO 81002

Consumer Products Safety Commission
Bureau of Compliance
5401 Westbard Avenue
Bethesda, MD 20207

Department of Agriculture
14th Street and Independence Avenue SW
Washington, DC 20250
(202) 447-2791

Scope of this office includes food safety and inspection, nutrition, veterinary medicine, consumer affairs.

Department of Commerce
14th Street and Constitution Avenue NW
Washington, DC 20230
(202) 377-2000

Covers subjects of engineering standards, imports and exports, minority-owned business, patents and trademarks, business outlook analyses, economic and demographic statistics.

Department of Defense
The Pentagon
Washington, DC 20301
(202) 545-6700

Covers mapping, nuclear operations and technology, foreign country security and atomic energy.

Department of Education
400 Maryland Avenue SW
Washington, DC 20202
(202) 732-3366

Scope includes bilingual and adult education, libraries, special education, educational statistics.

Department of Energy
Forrestal Building, 1000 Independence Avenue SW
Washington, DC 20585
(202) 586-5000

Areas covered are conservation, inventions, fusion and nuclear energy, coal, gas, shale and oil.

Department of Health and Human Services
200 Independence Avenue SW
Washington, DC 20201
(202) 245-7000

Information available on diseases, drug abuse and research, family planning, food safety, occupational safety, statistical data.

Department of Housing and Urban Development
451 7th Street SW
Washington, DC 20410
(202) 755-5111

Scope involves fair housing, energy conservation, urban studies and elderly housing.

Department of the Interior
18th and C Streets NW
Washington, DC 20240
(202) 343-7220

Covers the areas of water, natural resources, mapping, geology, fish and wildlife.

Department of Justice
10th Street and Constitution Avenue NW
Washington, DC 20530
(202) 633-2000

Concerned with civil rights, drug enforcement, prisons, antitrust and justice statistics.

Department of Labor
200 Constitution Avenue NW
Washington, DC 20210
(202) 523-6666

Divisions are concerned with labor-management relations, labor statistics, occupational safety and health, women's employment issues, productivity and technology.

Department of State
2201 C Street NW
Washington, DC 20520
(202) 647-4000

Covers international affairs involving diplomacy, arms, drugs, human rights.

Department of Transportation
400 7th Street SW
Washington, DC 20590
(202) 366-4000

Scope includes aviation, automobile, boat, rail and highway standards and safety.

Department of the Treasury
15th Street and Pennsylvania Avenue NW
Washington, DC 20220

Covers the areas of customs, taxpayer assistance, currency research, development and production.

Environmental Protection Agency
401 M Street SW
Washington, DC 20460
1 (800) 368-5888 except DC and VA
(703) 557-1938 in DC and VA

Federal Communications Commission (FCC)
1919 M Street NW
Washington, DC 20554
(202) 632-7000

Federal Trade Commission
Pennsylvania Avenue and 6th Street NW
Washington, DC 20580
(202) 326-2000

Food and Drug Administration
FDA Center for Food Safety and Applied Nutrition
200 Charles Street, SW
Washington, DC 20402

Library of Congress
Copyright Office
101 Independence Ave. SE
Washington, DC 20540
Public Information Office (202) 707-2100

Patent and Trademark Office
U.S. Department of Commerce
P.O. Box 9
Washington, DC 20231
Public Information Office (703) 557-4357

Superintendent of Documents
Government Printing Office
Washington, DC 20402

U.S. International Trade Commission
500 E Street SW
Washington, DC 20436

U.S. Small Business Administration
1441 L Street NW
Washington, DC 20005

The SBA offers an extensive selection of information on most business management topics from how to start a business to exporting your products. A free copy of the *Directory of Business Development Publications* can be obtained by contacting your local SBA office or by calling the Small Business Answer Desk at 1-800-827-5722.

The SBA has offices throughout the country. Consult the U.S. Government section in your telephone directory for the office nearest you. SBA offers a number of programs and services, including training and educational programs, counseling services, financial programs and contact assistance. Inquire at the SBA about the following:

Service Corp of Retired Executives (SCORE): This national organization, sponsored by SBA, is made up of volunteer business executives who provide free counseling, workshops and seminars to prospective and existing small business people.

Small Business Development Centers (SBDCs): Sponsored by the SBA in partnership with state and local governments, the educational community and the private sector. They provide assistance, counseling and training to prospective and existing business people.

Small Business Institutes (SBIs): Organized through SBA on more than 500 college campuses around the nation. The institutes provide counseling by students and faculty to small business clients.

For more information about SBA business development programs and services, call the SBA Small Business Answer Desk at 1-800-827-5722.

Software, Books and Publications

Software

Pinson, Linda and Jerry Jinnett. **Automate Your Business Plan,** Analytical Software Partners & Out of Your Mind...and Into the Marketplace™, 1993 (Software for IBM and Compatibles. Translates **Anatomy of a Business Plan** into a computer program. No other software needed. Full-powered word processor. Spreadsheets are preformatted and preformulated. Requires 640k internal memory.)

Books

Bangs, David. *The Cash Flow Control Guide.* Upstart, 1990.

Bangs, David. *The Market Planning Guide.* Upstart, 1989.

Bangs, David. *The Start Up Guide.* Upstart, 1989.

Bobrow, Edwin. *Pioneering New Products: A Market Survival Guide.* Dow Jones-Irwin, 1987.

Breen, George, and A. A. Blankenship. *Do it Yourself Marketing Research.* McGraw-Hill, 1982.

Clifford, Denis, and Ralph Warner. *The Partnership Book.* Nolo Press, 1989.

Colman, Bob. *Small Business Survival Guide.* W.W. Norton, 1987.

DuBoff, Leonard. *The Law (in Plain English) for Small Business.* Madrona Publications, 1987.

Dawson, George M. *Borrowing for Your Business.* Upstart, 1992.

Friedman, Robert. *The Complete Small Business Legal Guide.* Enterprise-Dearborn, 1993.

Hawkin, Paul. *Growing a Business.* Simon and Schuster, 1987.

Holtz, Herman. *Advice, a High Profit Business.* Prentice-Hall, 1986.

Husch, Tony, and Linda Foust. *That's a Great Idea*. Gravity Press, 1986.

Joseph, Richard, Anna Nekoranec and Carl Steffens. *How to Buy a Business*. Enterprise-Dearborn, 1993.

Lavin, Michael. *Business Information: How to Find It, How to Use It*. Oryx Press, 1987.

Levinson, Jay Conrad. *Guerrilla Marketing: Secrets for Making Big Profits from your Small Business*. Houghton-Mifflin, 1984.

Mathewson, G. Bradley. *Asking for Money: the Entrepreneur's Guide to the Financing Process*. Financial Systems Associates, 1989.

Moran, Peg. *Invest in Yourself: a Woman's Guide to Starting Her Own Business*. Doubleday, 1984.

Nicholas, Ted. *The Executive's Business Letters Book*. Enterprise-Dearborn, 1992.

Nicholas, Ted. *The Complete Guide to Business Agreements*. Enterprise-Dearborn, 1992.

Nicholas, Ted. *The Complete Book of Corporate Forms*. Enterprise-Dearborn, 1992.

Nicholas, Ted. *How To Get Your Own Trademark*. Enterprise-Dearborn, 1992.

Ogilvy, David. *Ogilvy on Advertising*. Crown Publishers, 1983.

Pinson, Linda, and Jerry Jinnett. *Steps to Small Business Start-Up*. Upstart, 1993.

Pinson, Linda, and Jerry Jinnett. *Target Marketing for the Small Business*. Upstart, 1993.

Pinson, Linda, and Jerry Jinnett. *Keeping the Books: Recordkeeping and Accounting for the Small Business*. Upstart, 1993.

Pinson, Linda, and Jerry Jinnett. *The Home-Based Entrepreneur*. Upstart, 1993.

Pinson, Linda, and Jerry Jinnett. *The Woman Entrepreneur*. Upstart, 1992.

Price Waterhouse Information Guides. *Doing Business In...* (various foreign countries).

Snowdon, Sondra. *The Global Edge: How Your Company Can Win in the International Marketplace*. Simon and Schuster, 1986.

Wilkens, Joanne. *Her Own Business: Success Secrets of Entrepreneurial Women*. McGraw-Hill, 1987.

Worthington, Anita, and Robert E. Worthington. *Staffing a Small Business: Hiring, Compensating, and Evaluating*. Oasis Books, 1987.

Zuckerman, Laurie. *On Your Own: A Woman's Guide to Building a Business*. Upstart, 1993.

BUSINESS MAGAZINES

Black Enterprise Magazine
130 Fifth Avenue
New York, NY 10011-4399

Business Week
1221 Avenue of the Americas
New York, NY 10020-1001
(212) 512-2511

Entrepreneur Magazine
2392 Morse Avenue
Irvine, CA 92714-5234
(714) 261-2325

Forbes
60 Fifth Avenue
New York, NY 10011-8865
1 (800) 888-9896

Home Office Computing
730 Broadway
New York, NY 10003
(212) 505-3580

Inc.
38 Commercial Wharf
Boston, MA 02110-8000
(617) 248-8000

Nation's Business
1615 H Street, N.W.
Washington, DC 20062-2000
(202) 463-5650

ORGANIZATIONS AND ASSOCIATIONS

American Management Association
135 West 50th Street
New York, NY 10020
(212) 586-8100

Offers management assistance, including home-study courses on audio-cassette.

American Marketing Association
250 S. Wacker Drive, Suite 200
Chicago, IL 60606
(312) 648-0536

Publishes annotated bibliographies on important marketing topics, conducts seminars and other educational programs.

National Federation of Independent Business
150 W. 20th Avenue
San Mateo, CA 94403
(415) 341-7441
     -or-
600 Maryland Ave. S.W., Suite 700
Washington, DC 20024
(202) 554-9000

Represents small business interests to state and federal governments, distributes educational information and publications, and holds conferences.

Association of Collegiate Entrepreneurs (ACE)
Young Entrepreneurs Organization (YEO)
342 Madison Ave., #1104
New York, NY 10173
(212) 922-0837

ACE members are student entrepreneurs, while YEO offers membership to non-student entrepreneurs under the age of 30. Hold regional and national conferences, publish a newsletter, and act as information clearing house for young entrepreneurs.

National Association of Women Business Owners (NAWBO)
1377 K Street NW, Suite 637
Washington, DC 20005
(301) 608-2590

Professional organization for women in business with more than 50 local chapters. Helps broaden opportunities for women in business by offering workshops, seminars and networking opportunities, providing information and referral services to members, maintaining a database of women-owned businesses and actively impacting legislation.

International Council for Small Business
US Association for Small Business and Entrepreneurs
905 University Avenue, Room 203
Madison, WI 53715
(608) 262-9982

Professional organization for educators and entrepreneurs interested in the development of small business.

APPENDIX

I

Glossary of Business and Financial Terms

The following glossary will define business and financial terms with which you may not be familiar. Use of these terms will help you to speak and write in a language that will be understood by potential lenders and investors as well as business associates with whom you may be dealing.

Glossary of Business and Financial Terms

Account: A separate record showing the increases and decreases in each asset, liability, owner's equity, revenue and expense item.

Accounting: The process by which financial information about a business is recorded, classified, summarized and interpreted by a business.

Accounting professional: One who is skilled at keeping business records. Usually, a highly trained professional rather than one who keeps books. An accountant can set up the books needed for a business to operate and help the owner understand them.

Accounts payable: A record of what you owe to your creditors for goods or services received.

Account receivable: A record of what is owed to your business as a result of extending credit to a customer who purchases your products or services. All of the credit accounts taken together are your "accounts receivable."

Amortization: To liquidate on an installment basis: the process of gradually paying off a liability over a period of time.

Analysis: Breaking an idea or problem down into its parts; a thorough examination of the parts of anything.

Asset: Anything of worth (having cash value) that is owned by your business (i.e., cash on hand, inventory, land, buildings, vehicles and equipment). Accounts receivable, notes receivable and prepaid purchases are also assets.

Articles of Incorporation: A legal document filed with the state which sets forth the purposes and regulations for a corporation. Each state has different regulations.

Bad debts: Money owed to you that you cannot collect.

Balance: The amount of money remaining in an account.

Balance sheet: An itemized statement that lists the total assets and the total liabilities of a given business to portray its net worth at a given moment in time.

Bookkeeping: The process of recording business transactions into the accounting records.

Break-even analysis: A method used to determine the point at which the business will neither make a profit nor incur a loss. That point is expressed in either the total dollars of revenue exactly offset by total expenses or in total units of production, the cost of which exactly equals the income derived by their sale.

Bottom line: A business's net profit or loss after taxes for a specific accounting period.

Budget: A plan expressed in financial terms. A business is then evaluated by measuring its performance in terms of these goals. The budget contains projections for cash inflow and outflow and other balance sheet items.

Business venture: Taking financial risks in a commercial enterprise.

Capital: Money available to invest or the total of accumulated assets available for production. See "Owner's Equity."

Capital equipment: Equipment that you use to manufacture a product, provide a service, or use to sell, store and deliver merchandise. Such equipment will not be sold in the normal course of business, but will be used and worn out or consumed in the course of business.

Capital expenditure: An expenditure for a purchase of an item of property, plant or equipment that has a useful life of more than one year (Fixed asset).

Cash: Money on hand or readily available.

Cash discount: A deduction that is given for prompt payment of a bill.

Cash flow: The actual movement of cash within a business; cash inflow minus cash outflow.

Cash receipts: The money received by a business from customers.

Collateral: Something of value given or held as a pledge that a debt or obligation will be fulfilled.

Contract: An agreement regarding mutual responsibilities between two or more parties.

Controllable expenses: Those expenses which can be controlled or restrained by the business person. Variable expenses.

Corporation: A voluntary organization of persons, either actual individuals or legal entities, legally bound together to form a business enterprise; an artificial legal entity created by government grant and treated by law as an individual.

Co-signers: Joint signers of a loan agreement, pledging to meet the obligations in case of default.

Cost of goods sold: The cost of inventory sold during an accounting period. It is equal to the beginning inventory for the period plus the cost of purchases made during the period minus the ending inventory for the period.

Creditor: A company or individual to whom a business owes money.

Current assets: Cash plus any assets that will be converted into cash within one year plus any assets that you plan to use up within one year.

Current liabilities: Debts that must be paid within one year.

Current ratio: A dependable indication of liquidity computed by dividing current assets by current liabilities. A ratio of 2.0 is acceptable for most businesses.

Depreciable base of an asset: The cost of an asset used in the computation of yearly depreciation expense.

Direct expenses: Those expenses that relate directly to your product or service.

Debt capital: The part of the investment capital that must be borrowed.

Debt: That which is owed.

Debt measures: The indication of the amount of other people's money that is being used to generate profits for a business. The more indebtedness, the greater the risk of failure.

Debt ratio: The key financial ratio used by creditors in determining how indebted a business is and how able it is to service the debts. The debt ratio is calculated by dividing total liabilities by total assets. The higher the ratio, the more risk of failure. The acceptable ratio is dependent upon the policies of your creditors and bankers.

Default: Failure to pay a debt or meet an obligation.

Depreciation: A decrease in value through age, wear or deterioration. Depreciation is a normal expense of doing business that must be taken into account. There are laws and regulations governing the manner and time periods that may be used for depreciation.

Expenses: The costs of producing revenue through the sale of goods or services.

Entrepreneur: An innovator of business enterprise who recognizes opportunities to introduce a new product, a new process or an improved organization, and who raises the necessary money, assembles the factors for production and organizes an operation to exploit the opportunity.

Equity: The monetary value of a property or business that exceeds the claims and/or liens against it by others.

Financial statements: The periodic reports that summarize the financial affairs of a business.

Fixed assets: Items purchased for use in a business that are depreciable over a fixed period of time determined by the expected useful life of the purchase. Usually includes land, buildings, vehicles and equipment not intended for resale. Land is not depreciable, but is a fixed asset.

Fixed expenses: Those costs that don't vary from one period to the next. Generally, these expenses are not affected by the volume of business.

Gross: Overall total revenues before deductions.

Gross profit on sales: The difference between net sales and the cost of goods sold.

Gross profit margin: An indicator of the percentage of each sales dollar remaining after a business has paid for its goods. It is computed by dividing the gross profit by the sales.

Horizontal analysis: A percentage analysis of the increases and decreases on the items on comparative financial statements. A horizontal financial statement analysis involves comparison of data for the current period with the same data of a company for previous periods. The percentage of increase or decrease is listed.

Income statement: A financial document that shows how much money (revenue) came in and how much money (expense) was paid out.

Interest: The cost of borrowing money. The price charged or paid for the use of money or credit.

Inventory: The stock of goods that a business has on hand for sale to its customers.

Invest: To lay out money for any purpose from which a profit is expected.

Invest measures: Ratios used to measure an owner's earnings for his or her investment in the company. See "Return on investment (ROI)."

Invoice: A bill for the sale of goods or services sent by the seller to the purchaser.

Lease: A long term rental agreement.

Liabilities: Amounts owed by a business to its creditors. The debts of a business.

Liability insurance: Risk protection for actions for which a business is liable.

Limited partnership: A legal partnership where some owners are allowed to assume responsibility only up to the amount invested.

Liquidate: To settle a debt or to convert to cash.

Liquidity: The ability of a company to meet its financial obligations. A liquidity analysis focuses on the balance sheet relationships for current assets and current liabilities.

Loan: Money lent at interest.

Long-term liabilities: Liabilities that will not be due for more than a year in the future.

Management: The art of conducting and supervising a business.

Marketing: All the promotional activities involved in the buying and selling of a product or service.

Merchandise: Goods bought and sold in a business. "Merchandise" or stock is a part of inventory.

Net income: The amount by which revenue is greater than expenses. On an income statement this is usually expressed as both a pre-tax and after-tax figure.

Net loss: The amount by which expenses are greater than revenue. On an income statement this figure is usually listed as both a pre-tax and after-tax figure.

Net profit margin: The measure of a business's success with respect to earnings on sales. It is derived by dividing the net profit by sales. A higher margin means the firm is more profitable.

Net worth: The owner's equity in a given business represented by the excess of the total assets over the total amounts owing to outside creditors (total liabilities) at a given moment in time. The net worth of an individual is determined by deducting the amount of all personal liabilities from the total of all personal assets.

Nonrecurring: One time, not repeating. "Nonrecurring" expenses are those involved in starting a business which only have to be paid once and will not occur again.

Note: A written promise with terms for payment of a debt.

Operating expenses: Normal expenses incurred in the running of a business.

Operating profit margin: The ratio representing the pure operations profits, ignoring interest and taxes. It is derived by dividing the income from operations by the sales. The higher the percentage of operating profit margin the better.

Other expenses: Expenses that are not directly connected with the operation of a business. The most common is interest income.

Other income: Income that is earned from nonoperating sources. The most common is interest income.

Owners' equity: The financial interest of the owner of a business. The total of all owner equity is equal to the business's assets minus its liabilities. The owners' equity represents total investments in the business plus or minus any profits or losses the business has accrued to date.

Partnership: A legal business relationship of two or more people who share responsibilities, resources, profits and liabilities.

Payable: Ready to be paid. One of the standard accounts kept by a bookkeeper is "accounts payable." This is a list of those bills that are current and due to be paid.

Personal financial history: A summary of personal financial information about the owner of a business. The personal financial history is often required by a potential lender or investor.

Prepaid expenses: Expense items that are paid for prior to their use. Some examples are insurance, rent, prepaid inventory purchases, etc.

Principal: The amount shown on the face of a note or a bond. Unpaid principal is the amount remaining at any given time.

Pro forma: A projection or estimate of what may result in the future from actions in the present. A pro forma financial statement is one that shows how the actual operations of the business will turn out if certain assumptions are achieved.

Profit: Financial gain; returns over expenditures. The sum remaining after deducting costs.

Profit margin: The difference between your selling price and all of your costs.

Profit & loss statement: A list of the total amount of sales (revenues) and total costs (expenses). The difference between revenues and expenses is your profit or loss. Income statement.

Quarterly budget analysis: A method used to measure actual income and expenditures against projections for the current quarter of the financial year and for the total quarters completed. The difference is usually expressed as the amount and percentage over or under budget.

Quick ratio: A test of liquidity subtracting inventory from current assets and dividing the result by current liabilities. A quick ratio of 1.0 or greater is usually recommended.

Ratio analysis: An analysis involving the comparison of two individual items on financial statements. One item is divided by the other and the relationship is expressed as a ratio.

Receivable: Ready for payment. When you sell on credit, you keep an "accounts receivable" as a record of what is owed to you and who owes it. In accounting, a "receivable" is an asset.

Retail business: A business that sells goods and services directly to individual consumers.

Retained earnings: Earnings of a corporation that are kept in the business and not paid out in dividends. This amount represents the accumulated, undistributed profits of the corporation.

Return on investment (ROI): The rate of profit an investment will earn. The ROI is equal to the annual net income divided by total assets. The higher the ROI, the better. Business owners should set a target for the ROI and decide what they want their investments to earn.

Revenue: The income that results from the sale of products or services or from the use of investments or property.

Service business: A business that provides services rather than products to its customers.

Share: One of the equal parts into which the ownership of a corporation is divided. A "share" represents a part ownership in a corporation.

Sole proprietorship: A legal structure of a business having one person as the owner.

Stock: Accumulated merchandise.

Stockholders' equity: The stockholders' shares of stock in a corporation plus any retained earnings.

Takeover: The acquisition of one company by another.

Tangible personal property: Machinery, equipment, furniture and fixtures not attached to the land.

Target market: The specific individuals, distinguished by socio-economic, demographic, and interest characteristics, who are the most likely potential customers for the goods and services of a business.

Terms of sale: The conditions concerning payment for a purchase.

Three-year projection: A pro forma (projected) income statement showing anticipated revenues and expenses for a business.

Trade credit: Permission to buy from suppliers on open account.

Unearned income: Revenue received, but not yet earned.

Variable costs: Expenses that vary in relationship to the volume of activity of a business.

Vertical analysis: A percentage analysis used to show the relationship of the components in a single financial statement. In vertical analysis of an income statement, each item on the statement is expressed as a percentage of net sales.

Volume: An amount or quantity of business; the "volume" of a business is the total it sells over a period of time.

Wholesale: Selling for resale.

Wholesale business: A business that sells its products to other wholesalers, retailers or volume customers at a discount.

Working capital: Current assets minus current liabilities. This is a basic measure of a company's ability to pay its current obligations.

APPENDIX

II

An Actual Business Plan

Marine Art of California
Written by
Robert Garcia

The business plan presented on the following pages is an actual business plan developed by a real business owner. It has been included in the book to help you with the writing of your business plan.

Bob Garcia of "Marine Art of California" wrote this plan in the summer of 1992. At that time he was in the process of organizing his business for startup and looking for investors in the form of limited partnerships. Mr. Garcia is now in business and has been updating his plan regularly to reflect what is actually happening in the operation of his venture.

As you proceed with the writing of your own plan, it may help you to look at Mr. Garcia's plan to see how he handled each of the corresponding sections. Some of the research material has been condensed and we have not included all of his supporting documents. All financials are projections because the business had no history for the development of a profit & loss statement or balance sheet. We have also chosen to omit his personal financial history.

We are very pleased that we have the opportunity to include this material in *Anatomy of a Business Plan*. We hope that it will be of benefit to you. We thank Bob Garcia for being so generous and for allowing us to share his interpretation of business planning with our readers.

MARINE ART OF CALIFORNIA

P.O. Box 10059-251
Newport Beach, CA 92658
(714) 722-6478

BUSINESS PLAN

Robert A. Garcia, President   (714) 722-6478
P.O. Box 10059-251
Newport Beach, CA 92658

Plan prepared September, 1992
by
Robert A. Garcia

(Private and Confidential)

MARINE ART OF CALIFORNIA

TABLE OF CONTENTS

MARINE ART OF CALIFORNIA

Statement of Purpose

Marine Art of California is a Limited Partnership to be established in 1992. The direct mail order and showroom company will be located in Newport Beach, CA. The company is seeking equity capital in the amount of $130,000 for the purpose of start-up operations and to cover estimated operating expenses for 6 months.

Funding is needed in time for the first catalog issue to be distributed in November and for a showroom to be operational in the same month for the Christmas buying season. There is a 2 to 3 week period between order placement and delivery date.

Repayment of the loan and interest can begin promptly within 30 days of receipt and can be secured by the percentage of the business to be held as collateral.

I. ORGANIZATIONAL PLAN

Description of Business

Marine Art of California is a start-up company in Newport Beach, marketing the works of California artists through a direct mail-order catalog. The product line is a unique combination of art, gift items and jewelry, all tied together by a marine or nautical theme. This marketing concept is a first! There is no known retailer or catalog company exclusively featuring the works of California artists in either a retail store or by mail-order catalog. I'm targeting a specific genre of the art market that, in terms of marketability, is on the cutting edge.

Having managed Sea Fantasies Art Gallery at Fashion Island Mall in Newport Beach from November 1990 to November 1991, I was able to discuss my idea personally and collect more than 700 names and addresses of highly interested customers who were marine art lovers. Of these, 90% lived in the surrounding communities and the rest came from across the U.S. and other nations.

Currently, I am mailing literature, taking orders and making sales. I have a large number of artists and vendors throughout California with marketing agreements already in place.

I have assets of about $10,000 of miscellaneous items. These include framed and unframed originals, lithographs, posters, bronzes, acrylic boats, jewelry, videos, cassettes, CDs, T-shirts, glass figurines, greeting cards, shells and coral.

Sales will be processed by a four-step marketing plan. First is a direct mail-order catalog published bi-monthly (six times a year). This allows for complete marketing freedom targeting high-income households, interior designers, and other businesses located in coastal areas. The second is to generate sales through a retail showroom where merchandise can be purchased on-site and large high-end pieces (exhibited on consignment) can be ordered by catalog and drop shipped from artist/vendor directly to the customer. Third, a comprehensive advertising campaign targeting the surrounding high income communities shall be conducted, e.g., Yellow Pages, high-profile magazines, monthly guest artist shows, Grand Opening mailings and fliers with discount coupons. Fourth is to conduct an ongoing telemarketing program aimed at customers on our mailing lists in our local area at minimal cost.

Industry trends have stabilized with the bottoming of the current recession. My plan to counter this situation is to obtain exclusive marketing rights on unique designs and the widest selection in the market of quality items priced affordably under $100.00.

My plan is to secure my ranking as the #2 marine art dealer in Southern California, second only to the Wyland Galleries by the end of 1994 and by 1995, through steadily increasing catalog distribution to more than 150,000 copies per mailing, to rank as the #1 dealer in California in gross sales! From 1995 through 1997, projected catalog distribution will increase at a rate of at least 100,000 catalogs per year.

Legal Structure

The structure of the company will consist of one (1) General Partner and up to twenty (20) Limited Partners. The amount of funds needed from the Limited Partners is $130,000, which will equal 45% ownership of the business. Each Limited Partner's investment of $6,500 shall equal 2.25% of the business.

The investment will be treated as a loan and will be paid back over 15 years at 11% interest. The loan repayment amount for each 2.25% share will be $78.00 per month.

No Limited Partner shall have any right to be active in the conduct of the Partnership's business or have the power to bind the Partnership with any contract, agreement, promise or undertaking.

Provisions for Exit and Dissolution of the Company

The duration of the Partnership is 4 years. The General Partner will have the option of buying out the Limited Partners at the end of 4 years for $3,250 for each 2.25% interest. The buyout will not affect the outstanding loan, but the General Partner will provide collateral equal to the loan balance. The value of the business will be used as that collateral.

The distribution of profits shall be made within 75 days of the end of the year. Each Limited Partner will receive 2.25% per share of investment on any profits over and above the following two months' operating expenses (January and February). This amount will be required to maintain operations and generate revenues necessary to keep the company solvent.

In the event of a loss, each Limited Partner will assume a 2.25% liability for tax purposes and no profits will be paid. The General Partner will assume 55% of the loss for tax purposes.

A Key Man Insurance Policy in the amount of $250,000 shall be taken out on the General Partner to be paid to the Limited Partners in the event of the General Partner's death. The policy will be divided among the Limited Partners according to their percentage of interest in the company.

* See Copy of Contract in Supporting Documents for remainder of details.

Products and Service

The product line of **MARINE ART OF CALIFORNIA** consists of hand-signed limited editions of bronzes, acrylics, lithographs and posters with certificates. Included are exclusive designs (covered by signed contracts) of (1) originals and prints, (2) glass figurines and (3) fine jewelry. Rounding out the line are ceramic figures, videos, cassettes, C.D.s, marine life books, nautical clocks, marine jewelry (14k gold, sterling silver, genuine gemstones) and many more gift items, as well as a specific line for children. The marketing areas covered are both Northern California and Southern California.

The suppliers are artists and vendors from throughout California. They number over 260! I chose them because they best express, artistically, the growing interest in the marine environment. However, due to catalog space, only 30 to 50 artists/vendors can be represented. The retail showroom will be able to accommodate more.

My framing source for art images is a wholesale operation in Fullerton that services many large accounts including Disney Studios.

With an extremely large artist/vendor pool to draw from, I virtually eliminate any supply shortage that cannot be replaced quickly. Also, my shipping policy specifies a maximum of 3 weeks delivery time for custom-made pieces such as limited edition bronzes that need to be poured at foundries. Almost all of my suppliers have been in business for years and understand the yearly marketing trends.

Management

At present, I, Robert A. Garcia, am sole proprietor. I possess a wealth of business environment experience as indicated on my resume. My first long-term job was in the grocery industry with Stater Bros. Markets. I worked from high school through college, rising to the position of second assistant manager. The most valuable experience I came away with was the ability to work cohesively with a variety of personalities in demanding customer situations. It was at this point that I learned the importance and value of the customer in American business. The customers' needs are placed first! They are the most important link in the chain.

With the opportunity for better pay and regular weekday hours, I left Stater Bros. for employment with General Dynamics Pomona Division. For the next eleven years I was employed in Production Control and earned the title of Manufacturing Coordinator, supervising a small number of key individuals. I was responsible for all printed circuit board assemblies fabricated in off-site facilities located in Arizona and Arkansas. My duties included traveling between these facilities as needed. On a daily basis, I interfaced with supporting departments of Engineering, Quality Assurance, Procurement, Shipping and Receiving, Inspection, Stockroom and Inventory Control, Data Control Center, Electronic Fabrication, Machine Shop and Final Assembly areas.

The programs involved were the Standard Missile (Surface to Air Weapon System), Phalanx Close I Weapons System, Stinger System, and Sparrow Missile. My group was responsible for all analysis reports for upper management, Naval personnel, and corporate headquarters in St. Louis, Missouri. Duties included: solving material shortages, scheduling work to be released to maintain starts and completions, and to drive all support departments to

Management (cont.)

meet Final Assembly needs for contract delivery. Problem solving was the name of the game. The importance of follow-up was critical. Three key concepts that we used as business guidelines were (1) production of a **QUALITY PRODUCT** (2) at a **COMPETITIVE PRICE** (3) delivered **ON SCHEDULE**.

I'm currently in contact on a regular basis with 8 advisors varying in backgrounds of marketing, advertising, corporate law, small business start-up, finance, direct mail-order business and catalog production. Two individuals are college professors with active businesses, one a publisher of my business plan reference book, and two are retired executives with backgrounds in marketing and corporate law involved in the SCORE program through the Small Business Administration (SBA). I meet with these two executives every week.

Pertinent Courses and Seminars Completed

College Course	Supervisorial Training	Mt. San Antonio College
College Course	Successful Business Writing	Mt. San Antonio College
Seminar	Producing a Direct Mail Catalog	Coastline Community College
Seminar	Business Taxes and Recordkeeping	SCORE Workshop
Seminar	Business Plan Road Map	SCORE Workshop

Note: See resume in Supporting Documents

Personnel

The total number of employees to be hired initially will be four. Interviews have been conducted for each position, and all are tentatively filled. I will be on the premises during all business hours for both retail and catalog ordering operations during the first month of business. It will be the owner's duty to hire the following employees:

1. **Store Manager** - part time - $11.00 per hour

2. **1st Asst. Manager** - part time - $9.00 per hour

3. **2nd Asst. Manager** - part time - $8.00 per hour

4. **Sales Consultant** - part time - $5.50 per hour

5. **Administrative Asst.** - part time - $10.00 per hour

Personnel (cont.)

TRAINING:

1. **All employees** will be cross-trained in the following areas:

   a. Knowledge of product line
   b. Daily Sales Reconciliation Report (DSR)
   c. Catalog order processing
   d. Familiarity with key suppliers
   e. Company policy regarding customer relations
   f. Charges - VISA/MasterCard

PERSONNEL DUTIES:

1. **Manager** - Reports directly to Owner

   a. Open store (Key) - dust and vacuum
   b. Write work schedule
   c. Verify previous day's sales figures
   d. Follow up on any problems of previous day
   e. Head biweekly wall-to-wall inventory
   f. Reconcile any business discrepancies
   g. Responsible for store and catalog operations
   h. Order inventory
   i. Have access to safe
   j. Process catalog orders
   k. Conduct telemarketing in spare time
   l. Authorize employee purchase program (EPP)

2. **Administrative Assistant** - Reports to Manager

   a. Open store (Key)
   b. Write work schedule
   c. Perform office functions
      (1) Daily Sales Reconciliation Report   (DSR)
      (2) Accounts Receivable   (A/R)
      (3) Accounts Payable   (A/P)
      (4) Payroll   (P/R)
      (5) General Ledger   (G/L)
      (6) Typing - 60 wpm
      (7) Computer - WP/Lotus/D-Base
      (8) 10-Key Adding Machine
   d. Have access to safe
   e. Process catalog orders
   f. Authorize employee purchase program (EPP)

Personnel (cont.)

3. **1st Assistant Manager** - Reports to Manager
   a. Close store (Key)
   b. Order inventory
   c. Complete Daily Sales Reconciliation Report (DSR)
   d. Follow up on day's problems not yet solved
   e. Have access to safe
   f. Process catalog orders
   g. Conduct telemarketing in spare time

4. **2nd Assistant Manager** - Reports to 1st Assistant Manager
   a. Is familiar with all 1st Assistant Manager tasks
   b. Process catalog orders
   c. Assist in Customer Relations follow-up
   d. Dust and vacuum showroom
   e. Conduct telemarketing in spare time

5. **Sales Consultant** - Reports to 2nd Assistant Manager
   a. Cover showroom floor
   b. Process catalog orders
   c. Assist in Customer Relations follow-up
   d. Dust and vacuum showroom
   e. Conduct telemarketing in spare time

EMPLOYEE PROFILE:

1. Personable, outgoing, reliable, in good health
2. College background
3. High integrity and dedication
4. Neat in appearance
5. Able to take on responsibilities
6. Able to follow directives
7. Demonstrates leadership qualities
8. Previous retail experience
9. Basic office skills
10. Sincere interest in marine art and environment
11. Likes water sports
12. Team worker

Methods of Recordkeeping

All bookkeeping activities shall be done by the Administrative Assistant. Financial Reports will be filed by John Horist, CPA. John has been a personal friend of mine for 5 years and brings more than 40 years experience in his field. His hourly fee is very reasonable.

I would like to point out the key areas of recordkeeping required in the business and explain the software to be used and why. The areas are as follows:

Mail Lists - List & Mail Plus Software from Avery. It stores, sorts and prints up to 64,000 addresses with no programming required. It contains predefined label formats, or I can create my own. Searching and extracting subsets of the mailing list is possible. It also checks for duplicate entries.

Labels - MacLabelPro Software from Avery. The features include preset layouts for Avery laser labels and dot matrix labels, drawing tools and graphic sizing, built-in clip art and easy mail merge.

Accounting - Sybiz Windows Accounting Software. This program automatically updates all accounts, customers, payroll, suppliers, inventory and ledgers in one step. Windows graphics, fonts and integration make it easy to use.

The simplicity and power of these reasonably-priced programs make them very attractive.

Insurance

Prospective Carrier:	**State Farm Insurance** 2610 Avon, Suite C Newport Beach, CA 92660 (714) 645-6000	
Agent:	**Kim Hiller**	
Type of Insurance:	Business/Personal: Deductible: Liability:	$150,000.00 $1,000.00 $1,000,000.00
Premium:	Annual Premium: **Monthly Premium:** Workers' Comp:	$3,100.00 **$258.00** 1.43 per/1K of Gross Payroll

(8)

Security

**PROBLEM SITUATIONS TO BE CONSIDERED
AND PROTECTIVE MEASURES TO BE USED:**

1. **Internal Theft** - Employee Dishonesty

   a. Shoplifting of store merchandise - 2 closed circuit monitoring cameras recording showroom activity each business day.

   b. Cash theft - $400 limit of cash on hand. Timely safe drops and daily maintenance of Daily Sales Reconciliation Report will balance cash with receipts.

   c. Falsifying receipts - DSR will detect discrepancies.

   d. Employee Purchase Plan - will reduce inclination to steal. Employee discount is 35% off retail price. Can purchase layaway (20% down - balance over 60 days) or by payroll deduction (deducted from each check over 4 pay periods). Processed by authorized personnel other than oneself (2 signatures required).

   e. Employee Orientation Program - will stress security procedures and employee integrity.

   f. Biweekly wall-to-wall inventory - will reveal any losses.

2. **External Theft** - Customer shoplifting or robbery

   a. Walk-in theft - 2 closed circuit monitoring cameras recording showroom activity each business day.

   b. Break-in theft - robbery - alarm system plus closed circuit monitoring cameras. All fine jewelry is displayed in locked cases, removed and stored in safe each night.

   c. Wall-to-wall biweekly inventory will reveal any merchandise loss.

II. MARKETING PLAN

Target Marketing

Who are my customers?

1. Profile:
   Economic level - middle to upper class.

   Psychological makeup - art lover, jewelry lover, fashion conscious, ocean lover, eclectic taste, college educated, discriminating buyer, upwardly mobile life-style.

   Age - 35 to 55.

   Sex - Male/Female.

   Income level - $75,000 and above.

   Habits - high-expense entertainment, travel, marine-oriented hobbies (shell/dolphin collectors, scuba diver, boat/yacht owner, etc.), patrons of performing arts, concerts and museums.

   Work - professional, business owners, business executives, middle management, interior designers.

   Shop - middle to high-profile retail establishments.

2. Location:
   Orange County - coastal areas - home value of $500,000 and above.

   San Francisco County, San Diego County, San Bernardino County

3. Market size:
   Mail list purchased through wholesale mail list companies. The consumer base will range from 20,000 to 100,000 in the first year of operations.

4. Competition:
   Minimal due to unique 2-pronged marketing concept of marketing exclusively California marine art, custom-designed jewelry and giftware by way of (1) direct mail-order catalog and (2) retail showroom. No known operation in either category.

5. Other factors:
   As acting distributor for several artists I am able to retain exclusive marketing rights and, in most cases, have contracted to purchase at **10 to 15% below published wholesale price lists.**

Competition

The two areas of competition to consider will be (1) competitors to the retail showroom and (2) competitors to the direct mail-order operation.

(1)   Competition to Retail Showroom

Following this page are attached Competition Evaluation Worksheets for each competitor within a radius of 3 miles of proposed store site.[1]   Retail Stores to be evaluated will have at least 1 of the 4 categories of my product line:

      A.   MARINE ART - Framed (custom) and framed
      B.   MARINE SCULPTING - Cast in bronze and acrylic
      C.   MARINE AND NAUTICAL GIFT ITEMS
      D.   MARINE AND CONTEMPORARY JEWELRY DESIGNS - Fine and fashion

(2)   Competition to Direct Mail-Order Catalog

After investigating scores of catalog companies across the nation for the past year and speaking to artists and vendors across the state of California, we are aware of only one mail-order company with a similar theme but with a very different line and profile than **Marine Art of California.**

Methods of Distribution

Two-Way Distribution Program

   A. Direct Mail-Order Catalog

      1. Catalog mailings are distributed through target marketing.
      2. Orders are processed via telephone (1-800 #) or by return mail-order forms, accepting checks, VISA/MC, or American Express.
      3. Shipping in most cases is done by the artist or vendor directly to the customer per my instructions. All other shipping is done by **Marine Art of California.**
      4. Shipping costs are indicated in the catalog for each item. The customer is charged for shipping costs to reimburse the vendor.
      5. UPS shipping is available throughout the United States.

---

[1] Supporting documents are not included in this sample.

Methods of Distribution (cont.)

B. Retail Showroom

1. All items shown in the catalog will be available for purchase in the retail store.
2. High-ticket items will be carried on consignment with previous agreements already made with individual artists.
3. General Catalogs will be displayed on an order counter for all products not stocked in the store and that can be shipped on request.
4. All large items will be delivered anywhere in Orange County **at no charge**.

Since I am dealing with more than 260 artists and vendors across the state there should be no problem with the availability of merchandise. I am only able to carry about 55 artists and vendors in the catalog. Most items can be ordered for the store and be in stock within a 2-3 day turnaround.

For more detailed information on shipping arrangements, please see copy of Terms and Conditions for Participants in Supporting Documents section.

Advertising

Pacific Bell:	Yellow/white pages - 1 line	No charge
	Bold - $5.00 extra each	

Pac Bell/Sammy	Sales order # N74717625 (8/21/92)	
740-5211	Business line installation	$70.45
	Monthly rate	$11.85
	DEADLINE - August 19, 1992 Cannot change without	
	$18.00 per month rate increase	
	Display - 1/4 column listing (per month)	$49.00
	(Yearly cost $588.00)	
	Disconnect w/message (new #) 1 year	No charge

Donnelly:	White pages - 1 line	No charge
1-800-834-8425	Yellow pages - 2 lines	No charge
	3 or more	$10.00
	1/2 add (per month)	$27.00
	DEADLINE - August 21 (30 days to cancel)	
	Change deadline - September 10	
	Deposit due September 1	$183.00
	Monthly rate	$91.50
	(Yearly cost $1098.00)	

Advertising (cont.)

Metropolitan Magazine: 757-1404	Circulation 40,000 **Monthly rate**	129.00

Kim Moore
4940 Campus Drive
Newport Beach,
CA 92660

California Riveria:
494-2659
Leslie
Box 536
Laguna Beach,
CA 92652

1/6 page (per month)	$300.00
Art charge - one time	$50.00
40% discount - new subscriber	
Can hold rate for 6 months (Reg. $575.00)	
Color (per month)	$600.00
Articles	No charge
Print month end	
Circulation 50,000 29K High Traffic	
21K Direct Mail (92660 - 92625)	

Grand Opening:

4 x 6 Postcard - color	$400.00
Catering	$200.00
Artist show	
Discount coupons	
Fliers	
Newspaper ads (OC Register - one time cost - $100)	

Orange County News: Will get advertising estimates after 6 months in business.
(714) 565-3881

Orange County Register: Monthly rate $100.00

Advertising (cont.)

DONNELLY LISTINGS: 1993

5 Categories:

      1. Art Dealer, Galleries
      2. Interior Designers and Decorators
      3. Framers
      4. Jewelers
      5. Gift Shops

1.   ART DEALERS: Original Art, Lithos, Posters, Custom Framing, Bronze & Acrylic Sculptings, Int. Designer Prices, Ask for Catalog

2.   INTERIOR DECORATORS & DESIGNERS:
Original Art, Lithos, Posters, Custom Framing, Bronze & Acrylic Sculptings, Dealer Prices, Ask for Catalog

3.   FRAMERS: Large Selection of California Marine Art, Coastal Scenes, Custom Framing, Matting, Ask for Mail-Order Catalog

4.   JEWELERS: Specialty, Marine/Nautical Custom Designs by California Artists, 14K Gold, Sterling, Gemstones, Ask for Catalog

5.   GIFT SHOPS: Unique Line of Marine/Nautical Gifts, Glass Figurines, Acrylic Boats, Clocks, Art, Jewelry, Bronzes, Ask for Catalog

(14)

Pricing

A.   **Purchasing** - As stipulated in my Terms and Conditions, I request a 10 - 15% discount off published wholesale prices from artists and vendors in lieu of a participation fee. In about 95% of all agreements made, I am receiving this important discount!

B.   **Catalog Pricing**

      1.   Non-Jewelry Items - To recover publication costs, I have "keystoned" (100% markup) all items plus an additional 10-50%. Keystoning is typical in the retail industry. The added margin will cover any additional shipping charges that may not be covered by the indicated shipping fee paid by the customer.

      2.   Jewelry Items - Typical pricing in the industry is "Key" plus 50% (150% markup) to triple "Key" (200% markup). My markup is "Key" plus 10-30% to stay competitive.

C.   **Store Pricing** - All items will be "Keystone" plus 10 - 20% to allow a good margin for sales on selected items.

D.   **Wholesale** - Mailings and advertising will target Interior Decorators and Designers. To purchase wholesale, one must present a copy of their ASID or ISID license number and order a minimum purchase of $500.00 or more. The discount will be 20% off retail price.

Below is a sample of the computer data base with 17 fields of information on each item in inventory and how the retail price is computed.

File: Price List
Record 1 of 49

Item:	Fisherman's Wharf
Make:	Poster
Vendor:	A Chrasta
Exclusive:	So California
Size:	21.5 26 Sq
Vendor #:	NAC102WM
Image Pr:	$5.00
Type:	Poster
Frame:	PT4XW
Frame Price:	$31.50
Whsl. Price:	$36.50
Disc:	50% IM
Adj. Whsl:	$36.50
Key+:	10%
Retail Price:	$79.50
Group:	1

(15)

Gallery Design

After managing Sea Fantasies Gallery at Fashion Island Mall in Newport Beach during 1992, I have decided to recreate its basic layout. My goal is to create the most stunning and unique showroom design in Orange County with a product line that appeals to the high-profile customer's taste.

The design theme is to give the customer a feeling of being underwater when they enter. This would be accomplished by the use of glass display stands, live potted tropical plants to simulate lush, green underwater vegetation. Overhead curtains 18 inches wide would cleverly hide the track lighting while reflecting the light on the curtain sides, creating the illusion of an underwater scene with sunlight reflecting on the ocean surface.

A large-screen TV would continuously play videos of colorful underwater scenes with mood music playing on the store's sound system. A loveseat for shoppers to relax in would face the screen. Along with creating a soothing and relaxing atmosphere, the videos, CDs and cassettes would be available for sale. All fine art pieces (bronzes and framed art) would be accented with overhead track lighting, creating a strong visual effect.

Large coral pieces would be used for display purposes, such as for jewelry. Others would be strewn around the showroom floor area for a natural ocean floor effect.

Certain end displays would be constructed of glass with ocean floor scenes set inside consisting of an arrangement of coral, shells, and brightly painted wooden tropical fish on a two-inch bed of sand! All display stands would be available for sale.

This design concept was generally considered to be the most outstanding original store plan in Fashion Island as expressed by Mall customers and the Management Office. By incorporating these tried and proven concepts with my own creative designs, this gallery will have the most outstanding and unique appearance of any gallery from Long Beach to San Clemente.

The showroom area will be approximately 800 suare feet. The rear and stock area is about 200 square feet.

Timing of Market Entry

Considering the fact that most of my product line could be viewed as gift items, the upcoming Holiday Season is of **<u>CRITICAL IMPORTANCE!</u>** This is typically the peak sales period in the retail industry. Catalogs from large retailers and mail-order houses are already appearing in the mail for the holidays. These are the dates to consider:

1. **OCTOBER 8:**   Camera-ready artwork goes to film separator.

    Turnaround time - 3 days!

2. **OCTOBER 11:**   All slides and artwork must be ready to be delivered to the printer, Bertco Graphics, in Los Angeles.

    Turnaround time - 11 working days!

3. **OCTOBER 22:**   Printed catalogs must be delivered to Towne House Marketing in Santa Ana.

    Turnaround time - 3 days!

4. **OCTOBER 29:**   Catalogs shipped to Santa Ana Main Post Office.

    Turnaround time - 2 working days!

5. **NOVEMBER 1:**   **CUSTOMER RECEIVES CATALOG-** Ordering begins.

6. **DECEMBER 4:**   Last ordering date to ensure Christmas delivery! Can send via Federal Express all stocked items and all stocked items at vendors.

    Problem Items:
    a) High-end cast bronzes
    b) Hand-made glass figurines
    c) Oringinal paintings

    Turnaround time - 3 weeks!

(17)

Location

The prime business location targeted for **Marine Art of California** retail showroom is 1000 square feet at 106 Bayview Circle, Newport Beach, CA 92660. This site was chosen because of large front display windows, excellent visibility and access for the showroom, as well as adequate floor space to house inventory for catalog shipping. Both operations require certain square footage to operate successfully. Demographics and surrounding stores are extremely favorable.

Proposed site: Newport Beach, California

Features: *   Retail Shop space of 1000 sq. ft.
    *   Located in the primary retail and business sector of Newport Beach, Orange County's most affluent and growing community
    *   Excellent visibility and access
    *   Median household income in 1 mile radius is $90,000.00

Demographics[2]	**1 Mile**	**3 Miles**	**5 Miles**
Population:	1,043	111,983	308,906
Income:	$90,000	$61,990	$59,600

1991 Private Sector Employment (Daytime pop.)

1 Mile	**3 Miles**	**5 miles**
43,921	113,061	306,313

1991 Socio-Economic Status Indicator (SESI)

1 Mile	**3 Miles**	**5 Miles**
73	79	79

1991 Population by Age

1 Mile		**3 Miles**	**5 Miles**
	25 - 29	9.2%	8.4%
	30 - 34	9.4%	9.9%
	35 - 44	16.10%	18.6%
	45 - 54	12.3%	12.1%
	25 - 54	TOTAL 47.0%	49.0%

Leasing Agent: Chuck Sullivan
    CB Commercial
    4040 MacArthur Blvd
    Newport Beach CA 92660
    (714) 955-6431

---

[2] 1991 Donnelly Marketing Information Services

Industry Trends

Information extracted from: ABI/INFORM DATABASE at UCI Library for Business Research.

Title: **Sharper Image Revamps Product Line. Sells Items Consumers Can Actually Buy.**
Journal: **Marketing News** Vol: 26 Issue: 10 Date: May 11, 1992 Pg: 2
Summary: Although shoppers will still find upscale items at Sharper Image, the company has doubled the amount of goods that are more affordable. The addition of low-priced items is part of a continuing shift that will last, even if the economy improves.

Title: **What's Selling, and Why**
Journal: **Catalog Age** Vol: 9 Issue: 5 Date: May 1992 Pg: 5
Summary: Market researcher Judith Langer believes today's mailers must create a value package that combines quality and price. Merchandise is reflecting consumer sentiment about the economy and the desire to buy U.S. goods and services.

Title: **Tripping the Gift Market Fantastic**
Journal: **Catalog Age** Vol: 9 Issue: 6 Date: June 1992 Pg: 30
Summary: Christmas Fantastic and Celebration Fantastic catalogs feature gifts and decorative accessories and target upscale females age 25 and over. Response has been strong. Average orders of $95.00 for Christmas Fantastic and $85.00 for Celebration Fantastic have surpassed company expectations.

Title: **Spring Sales Blossom**
Journal: **Catalog Age** Vol: 9 Issue: 6 Date: June 1992 Pg: 36
Summary: Spring sales appear to be much stronger than in 1991. Many mailers believe the latest upturn in sales will be long-lasting.

Title: **Your Catalog's List Is Its Greatest Asset**
Journal: **Target Marketing** Vol: 15 Issue: 2 Date: February 1992 Pg: 44-45
Summary: There are a number of reasons why greater attention should be paid to the customer mail list rather than prospecting for new customers: 1. It is the primary source of profit for the company. 2. It is the cataloger's most valuable asset. 3. It will outperform a rented list by as much as 10 times in response rate and average order.

Note: The above articles have been condensed for brevity.

Publications and Services Utilized

Art Business News (Monthly)
>   Monthly trade magazine for art dealers and framers. Foremost business journal in the art industry. It provided readers with a wide range of art industry news, features, sales and marketing trends, and new product information. Reports on trade shows nationally and internationally.

National Jeweler (Monthly)
>   Dealer magazine. Provides jewelry industry news, features, sales and marketing trends, fashions and styles. Lists major manufacturers and wholesalers.

Catalog Age (Monthly)
>   Monthly journal featuring articles on mail-order companies. Provides inside information on statistics for mail-order business. Highly informative.

Target Marketing (Monthly) - Monthly trade journal.

Orange County Business Journal (Weekly)

Small Business Administration
Free Publications: **Selling by Mail Order**
                       Tax & Regulatory Requirements in Orange County
                       Partnership Agreements - Planning Checklist
                       Understanding Cash Flow
                       Developing A Strategic Business Plan
                       Insurance Checklist for Small Business

Anatomy of a Business Plan - Pinson & Jinnett (Dearborn Financial Publishing)

Direct Marketing Handbook - Edward L. Nash (McGraw-Hill)

The Catalog Handbook - James Holland

Direct Marketing Association - Membership organization for catalogers.

ABI/INFORM Data Base - University of California, Irvine (see Industry Trends section)
>   Online database located in the library. Contained in this database are abstracts and indexes to business articles published in more than 800 different journals. ABI/ INFORM is an excellent source of information on:

Companies	Trends	Marketing & Advertising
Products	Corporate Strategies	
Business Conditions	Management Strategies	

Orange County Demographic Overview - Demographic reports, charts and maps provided by the the market research department of the **Orange County Register**.

III. FINANCIAL DOCUMENTS

Summary of Financial Needs

I. **Marine Art of California,** a limited partnership, is seeking equity capital for start-up purposes.

  A. Direct Mail-Order Catalog

  B. Retail/Wholesale Showroom

II. **Funds needed to accomplish above goal** will be $130,000.00. See "Loan Fund Dispersal Statement" for distribution of funds and backup statement.

Loan Fund Dispersal Statement

I. **DISPERSAL OF LOAN FUNDS**
  Marine Art of California will utilize funds in the amount of $130,000.00 for start-up of two retail functions: (1) A direct mail-order catalog and (2) a retail showroom to conduct related functions.

II. **BACKUP STATEMENT**

Direct mail-order catalog:
  a) 24 pages
  b) 2 editions
  c) Quantities: 20K: **$20,000.00**
           30K: **23,200.00**

Start-up expense of warehouse - One Time Cost: **25,275.00**

3-Month Operating Expense: **58,364.00**
3-Month Total Loan Repayment Cost: **3,161.00**
  (@ $1,560.00 per month)

_____

                    TOTAL: **$130,000.00**

Catalog revenues will result in a net profit sufficient to pay all expenses and loan payments beginning in 30 days and continuing.

PRO FORMA CASH FLOW STATEMENT
page 1

	Pre-Start-up	NOV	DEC	1992 TOTALS	1993 JAN	FEB	MAR
1. CASH ON HAND (Beginning of Month)		84,725.00	86,152.00	84,725.00	71,575.00	59,312.00	42,837.00
2. CASH RECEIPTS							
A. Cash Sales		24,192.00	17,428.00	41,620.00	22,065.00	16,040.00	42,350.00
B. Collections from Credit Accounts							
C. Loan or Other Cash Injection	130,000.00						
3. TOTAL CASH RECEIPTS (A+B+C)	130,000.00	24,192.00	17,428.00	41,620.00	22,065.00	16,040.00	42,350.00
4. TOTAL CASH AVAILABLE	130,000.00	108,917.00	103,580.00	126,345.00	93,640.00	75,352.00	85,187.00
5. CASH PAID OUT							
A. Inventory Purchases	6,000.00	13,910.00	9,990.00	23,900.00	12,213.00	9,200.00	22,375.00
B. Gross Wages (Excludes withdrawals)		2,560.00	2,560.00	5,120.00	2,560.00	2,560.00	2,560.00
C. Payroll Expenses (Taxes, etc.)		192.00	192.00	384.00	192.00	192.00	192.00
D. Outside Services		0.00		0.00			
E. Catalog Expense	20,000.00		11,600.00	11,600.00	11,600.00	12,800.00	12,800.00
F. Advertising	600.00	221.00	221.00	442.00	221.00	221.00	221.00
G. Repairs and Maintenance		30.00	30.00	60.00	30.00	30.00	30.00
H. Supplies (Office & Operating)		300.00	300.00	600.00	300.00	300.00	300.00
I. Car, Delivery, and Travel		100.00	100.00	200.00	100.00	100.00	100.00
J. Shipping		400.00	400.00	800.00	400.00	400.00	400.00
K. Accounting and Legal	500.00	160.00	160.00	320.00	160.00	160.00	160.00
L. Rent	1,300.00	1,300.00	1,300.00	2,600.00	1,300.00	1,300.00	1,300.00
M. Telephone	50.00	500.00	500.00	1,000.00	600.00	600.00	700.00
N. Utilities (Alarm & Electric)	50.00	290.00	290.00	580.00	290.00	290.00	290.00
O. Insurance (Workers' Comp)	300.00	302.00	302.00	604.00	302.00	302.00	302.00
P. Taxes (Real Estate, etc.)		0.00	0.00	0.00	0.00	0.00	0.00
Q. Interest			1,286.00	1,286.00	1,286.00	1,286.00	1,286.00
R. Licenses and Permits	175.00			0.00			
S. Unexpected Expenditures	2,000.00	500.00	500.00	1,000.00	500.00	500.00	500.00
U. SUBTOTAL	30,975.00	20,765.00	29,731.00	50,496.00	32,054.00	30,241.00	43,516.00
V. Loan Principal Payment			274.00	274.00	274.00	274.00	274.00
W. (a) Capital Purchases - Office	9,000.00			0.00			
W. (b) Capital Purchases - Showroom	5,300.00			0.00			
X. Other Start-up Cost				0.00			
Y. Reserve and/or Escrow (Specify)				0.00			
Z. Owner's Withdrawal (includes life insurance)		2,000.00	2,000.00	4,000.00	2,000.00	2,000.00	2,000.00
6. TOTAL CASH PAID OUT	45,275.00	22,765.00	32,005.00	54,770.00	34,328.00	32,515.00	45,790.00
7. CASH POSITION (End of Mo.)	84,725.00	86,152.00	71,575.00	71,575.00	59,312.00	42,837.00	39,397.00
ESSENTIAL OPERATING DATA (Non-cash flow information)							
A. Sales Volume (Dollars)							
B. Accounts Receivable (End of Month)							
C. Bad Debt (EOM)							
D. Inventory (EOM)							
E. Accounts Payable (EOM)							
F. Depreciation - 20% @ 5 yrs							

PRO FORMA CASH FLOW STATEMENT
page 2

APR	MAY	JUN	JUL	AUG	SEP	OCT	NOV	DEC	1993 TOTAL
39,397.00	25,807.00	29,559.00	21,462.00	30,996.00	26,287.00	25,992.00	13,772.00	54,527.00	71,575.00
30,300.00	67,744.00	47,696.00	83,508.00	58,672.00	67,950.00	47,700.00	154,200.00	105,700.00	743,925.00
30,300.00	67,744.00	47,696.00	83,508.00	58,672.00	67,950.00	47,700.00	154,200.00	105,700.00	743,925.00
69,697.00	93,551.00	77,255.00	104,970.00	89,668.00	94,237.00	73,692.00	167,972.00	160,227.00	815,500.00
16,375.00	35,122.00	25,123.00	43,054.00	30,661.00	35,275.00	25,150.00	78,375.00	54,125.00	387,048.00
2,560.00	3,520.00	3,520.00	3,520.00	3,520.00	3,520.00	3,520.00	3,520.00	3,520.00	38,400.00
192.00	269.00	269.00	269.00	269.00	269.00	269.00	269.00	269.00	2,920.00
									0.00
16,600.00	16,600.00	18,400.00	18,400.00	20,200.00	20,200.00	22,000.00	22,000.00	22,000.00	213,600.00
521.00	521.00	521.00	521.00	521.00	521.00	521.00	521.00	521.00	5,352.00
30.00	30.00	30.00	30.00	30.00	30.00	30.00	30.00	30.00	360.00
300.00	300.00	300.00	300.00	300.00	300.00	300.00	300.00	300.00	3,600.00
100.00	100.00	100.00	100.00	100.00	100.00	100.00	100.00	100.00	1,200.00
400.00	400.00	400.00	400.00	400.00	400.00	400.00	400.00	400.00	4,800.00
160.00	160.00	160.00	160.00	160.00	160.00	160.00	160.00	160.00	1,920.00
1,300.00	1,300.00	1,300.00	1,300.00	1,300.00	1,300.00	1,300.00	1,300.00	1,300.00	15,600.00
700.00	1,000.00	1,000.00	1,250.00	1,250.00	1,500.00	1,500.00	1,800.00	1,800.00	13,700.00
290.00	290.00	290.00	290.00	290.00	290.00	290.00	290.00	290.00	3,480.00
302.00	320.00	320.00	320.00	320.00	320.00	320.00	320.00	320.00	3,768.00
0.00	0.00	0.00	0.00	0.00	0.00	0.00	0.00	0.00	0.00
1,286.00	1,286.00	1,286.00	1,286.00	1,286.00	1,286.00	1,286.00	1,286.00	1,286.00	15,432.00
									0.00
500.00	500.00	500.00	500.00	500.00	500.00	500.00	500.00	500.00	6,000.00
41,616.00	61,718.00	53,519.00	71,700.00	61,107.00	65,971.00	57,646.00	111,171.00	86,921.00	717,180.00
274.00	274.00	274.00	274.00	274.00	274.00	274.00	274.00	274.00	3,288.00
									0.00
									0.00
									0.00
									0.00
2,000.00	2,000.00	2,000.00	2,000.00	2,000.00	2,000.00	2,000.00	2,000.00	2,000.00	24,000.00
43,890.00	63,992.00	55,793.00	73,974.00	63,381.00	68,245.00	59,920.00	113,445.00	89,195.00	744,468.00
25,807.00	29,559.00	21,462.00	30,996.00	26,287.00	25,992.00	13,772.00	54,527.00	71,032.00	71,032.00
									0.00
									0.00
									0.00
									0.00
									2,860.00

(23)

QUARTERLY BUDGET ANALYSIS

For the Quarter Ending: March 31, 1993   ***YTD = year-to-date**

BUDGET ITEM	AMOUNT BUDGETED	ACTUAL THIS QUARTER	VARIATION THIS QUARTER	YTD BUDGET	ACTUAL YTD	VARIATION YTD
SALES REVENUES	80,455.00					
Less Inventory Purchases	43,788.00					
GROSS PROFIT	36,667.00					
EXPENSES						
1. Gross Wages (Excl. W/Drawels)	7,680.00					
2. Payroll Expenses (Taxes, etc.)	576.00					
3. Outside Services	0.00					
4. Catalog Expense	37,200.00					
5. Advertising	663.00					
6. Repairs & Maintenance	90.00					
7. Supplies (Office and Operating)	900.00					
8. Car, Delivery and Travel	300.00					
9. Shipping	1,200.00					
10. Accounting & Legal	480.00					
11. Rent	3,900.00					
12. Telephone	1,900.00					
13. Utilities (Alarm & Electric)	870.00					
14. Insurance (Workers' Comp.)	906.00					
15. Taxes	0.00					
16. Interest	3,858.00					
17. Licenses & Permits	0.00					
18. Unexpected Expenditures	1,500.00					
TOTAL EXPENSES (1 through 18)	62,023.00					
NET PROFIT (LOSS) BEFORE TAXES (Gross Profit less Total Expenses)	(25,356.00)					
NON-INCOME STATEMENT ITEMS						
1. Capital Purchases	0.00					
2. Loan Repayments	822.00					
3. Owner's Withdrawals	6,000.00					
CASH POSITION (Beg. of Quarter)	71,575.00					
CASH POSITION (End of Quarter)	39,397.00					

THREE-YEAR INCOME PROJECTION

	1992 NOV/DEC	% INC	1993 YEAR 1	% INC	1994 YEAR 2	% INC	1995 YEAR 3
Income:							
1. Net Sales (Gross - Ret & Allow)	**41,620.00**		**743,925.00**		**2,651,856.00**		**4,515,406.00**
a. Catalog Sales	33,820.00		672,925.00	26%	2,570,200.00	58%	4,421,500.00
b. Showroom Sales	4,600.00		46,325.00	15%	53,274.00	15%	61,266.00
c. Wholesale Sales	3,200.00		24,680.00	15%	28,382.00	15%	32,640.00
2. Cost of Goods Sold	**23,900.00**		**375,048.00**		**1,329,476.00**		**2,261,783.00**
a. Inventory (Jan 1)	6,000.00		6,000.00		18,000.00		25,000.00
b. Purchases - Catalog	19,600.00		336,460.00		1,285,100.00		2,210,750.00
Showroom (Walk-in)	2,300.00	12K	35,163.00	7K	33,637.00	7K	37,633.00
Wholesale	2,000.00		15,425.00		17,739.00		20,400.00
c. Cost of goods avail. for sale (a+b)	29,900.00		393,048.00		1,354,476.00		2,293,783.00
d. Deduct Inventory for Dec. 31	6,000.00	12K	18,000.00	7K	25,000.00	7K	32,000.00
3. Gross Profit on Sales	**17,720.00**		**368,877.00**		**1,322,380.00**		**2,253,623.00**
Expenses:							
1. Selling Expenses (Direct or Controllable)							
a. Gross Wages	5,120.00		38,400.00	7%	41,088.00	7%	43,964.16
b. Payroll Expenses	384.00		2,920.00	7%	3,124.40	7%	3,343.11
c. Advertising	1,042.00		5,352.00	7%	5,726.64	7%	6,127.50
d. Catalog Expense	31,600.00		213,600.00		694,400.00		1,272,000.00
e. Car, Delivery & Travel	200.00		1,200.00	7%	1,284.00	7%	1,373.88
f. Shipping	800.00		4,800.00	10%	5,280.00	10%	5,808.00
g. Accounting & Legal	820.00		1,920.00	7%	2,054.40	7%	2,198.21
h. Capital Purchases	14,300.00		0.00		0.00		0.00
i. Misc. Direct Expense	3,000.00		6,000.00	5%	6,300.00	5%	6,615.00
2. Administrative Expense (Indirect, Fixed)							
a. Supplies (Office & Operating)	600.00		3,600.00	7%	3,852.00	7%	4,121.64
b. Repairs & Maintenance	60.00		360.00	7%	385.20	7%	412.16
c. Rent	3,900.00		15,600.00	7%	16,692.00	7%	17,860.44
d. Telephone	1,050.00		13,700.00	10%	15,070.00	10%	16,577.00
e. Utilities (Alarm & Electric)	630.00		3,480.00	7%	3,723.60	7%	3,984.25
f. Insurance (+ Workers' Comp)	904.00		3,768.00	7%	4,031.76	7%	4,313.98
g. Misc. Indirect Expense	175.00		0.00	5%	0.00	5%	0.00
Total Expenses	**64,585.00**		**314,700.00**		**803,012.00**		**1,388,699.34**
Income From Operations (Income less Expenses)	(46,865.00)		54,177.00		519,368.00		864,923.66
Other Income - Interest Income	0.00		0.00		0.00		0.00
Other Expense - Interest Expense	1,286.00		15,432.00		15,432.00		15,432.00
Net Profit (Loss) Before Income Taxes	**(48,151.00)**		**38,745.00**		**503,936.00**		**849,491.66**
Income Taxes (26%)	0.00		10,073.70		131,023.36		220,867.83
Net Profit (Loss) After Income Taxes	**(48,151.00)**		**28,671.30**		**372,912.64**		**628,623.83**

(25)

BREAK-EVEN ANALYSIS

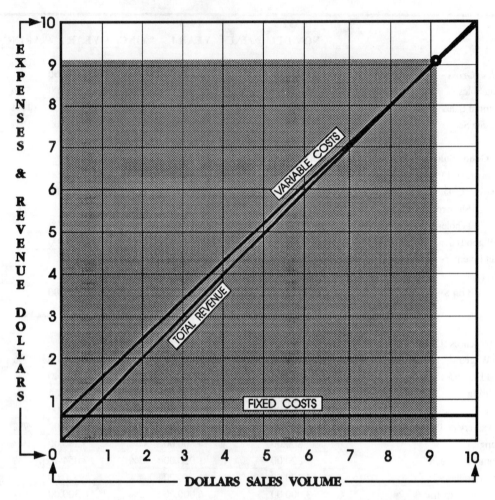

Note: Figures shown in hundreds of thousands of dollars (Ex: 2 = $200,000)

$$\text{B-E Point (Sales)} = \text{Fixed Costs} + \left[\frac{\text{Variable Costs}}{\text{Estimated Revenues}} \times \text{Sales} \right]$$

$$\text{B-E Point (Sales)} = \$64,545.00 + \left[\frac{\$730,406.00}{\$785,545.00} \times S \right]$$

$$\text{B-E Point (Sales)} = \$64,545.00 + \left[.929 \times S \right]$$

$$S = \$64,545.00 + .929\,S$$

$$S - .929\,S = \$64,545.00$$

$$.071\,S = \$64,545.00$$

$$S = \frac{\$64,545.00}{.071}$$

Break-Even Point
$$S = \$909,084.00$$

OPERATING PLAN FORECAST (P & L Projection)

SBA FORM 1099 (8-85) SOP: 60 10

page 1

	Month 1	NOV		Month 2	DEC		1992 Totals	Month 1	JAN	
REVENUE (Sales)	Estimate	Actual	%	Estimate	Actual	%		Estimate	Actual	%
Catalog Sales (60% - 40%)	20,292.00			13,528.00			33,820.00	18,900.00		
Showroom Sales (Walk-in)	2,300.00			2,300.00			4,600.00	1,725.00		
Wholesale Sales	1,600.00			1,600.00			3,200.00	1,440.00		
TOTAL REVENUES (Sales)	24,192.00	0.00	0.00	17,428.00	0.00	0.00	41,620.00	22,065.00	0.00	0.00
COST OF SALES										
Catalog Goods (50%)	11,760.00			7,840.00			19,600.00	9,450.00		
Showroom Sales (50%) 1993+$1K p/m	1,150.00			1,150.00			2,300.00	1,863.00		
Wholesale Sales (x .625)	1,000.00			1,000.00			2,000.00	900.00		
TOTAL COST OF SALES	13,910.00	0.00	0.00	9,990.00	0.00	0.00	23,900.00	12,213.00	0.00	0.00
GROSS PROFIT	10,282.00	0.00	0.00	7,438.00	0.00	0.00	17,720.00	9,852.00	0.00	0.00
EXPENSES										
Salary Expense	2,560.00			2,560.00			5,120.00	2,560.00		
Payroll Expense	192.00			192.00			384.00	192.00		
Outside Services	0.00			0.00			0.00	0.00		
Catalog Expense	0.00			11,600.00			11,600.00	11,600.00		
Advertising	221.00			221.00			442.00	221.00		
Repairs and Maintenance	30.00			30.00			60.00	30.00		
Supplies (Office & Operating)	300.00			300.00			600.00	300.00		
Car, Delivery, and Travel	100.00			100.00			200.00	100.00		
Shipping	400.00			400.00			800.00	400.00		
Accounting and Legal	160.00			160.00			320.00	160.00		
Rent	1,300.00			1,300.00			2,600.00	1,300.00		
Telephone	500.00			500.00			1,000.00	600.00		
Utilities (Alarm & Electric)	290.00			290.00			580.00	290.00		
Insurance (Workers' Comp)	302.00			302.00			604.00	302.00		
Taxes (Real Estate, etc)	0.00			0.00			0.00	0.00		
Interest ($1285.21)	0.00			1,286.00			1,286.00	1,286.00		
Miscellaneous	500.00			500.00			1,000.00	500.00		
TOTAL EXPENSES	6,855.00	0.00	0.00	19,741.00	0.00	0.00	26,596.00	19,841.00	0.00	0.00
NET PROFIT	3,427.00	0.00	0.00	(12,303.00)	0.00	0.00	(8,876.00)	(9,989.00)	0.00	0.00

OPERATING PLAN FORECAST (P & L Projection)

SBA FORM 1099 (8-85) SOP: 60 10

page 2

Month 2	FEB		Month 3	MAR		Month 4	APR		Month 5	MAY	
Estimate	Actual	%	Estimate	Actual	%	Estimate	Actual	%	Estimate	Actual	%
12,600.00			38,250.00			25,500.00			62,244.00		
2,000.00			2,500.00			3,000.00			3,500.00		
1,440.00			1,600.00			1,800.00			2,000.00		
16,040.00	0.00	0.00	42,350.00	0.00	0.00	30,300.00	0.00	0.00	67,744.00	0.00	0.00
6,300.00			19,125.00			12,750.00			31,122.00		
2,000.00			2,250.00			2,500.00			2,750.00		
900.00			1,000.00			1,125.00			1,250.00		
9,200.00	0.00	0.00	22,375.00	0.00	0.00	16,375.00	0.00	0.00	35,122.00	0.00	0.00
6,840.00	0.00	0.00	19,975.00	0.00	0.00	13,925.00	0.00	0.00	32,622.00	0.00	0.00
2,560.00			2,560.00			2,560.00			3,520.00		
192.00			192.00			192.00			269.00		
0.00			0.00			0.00			0.00		
12,800.00			12,800.00			16,600.00			16,600.00		
221.00			221.00			521.00			521.00		
30.00			30.00			30.00			30.00		
300.00			300.00			300.00			300.00		
100.00			100.00			100.00			100.00		
400.00			400.00			400.00			400.00		
160.00			160.00			160.00			160.00		
1,300.00			1,300.00			1,300.00			1,300.00		
600.00			700.00			700.00			1,000.00		
290.00			290.00			290.00			290.00		
302.00			302.00			302.00			320.00		
0.00			0.00			0.00			0.00		
1,286.00			1,286.00			1,286.00			1,286.00		
500.00			500.00			500.00			500.00		
21,041.00	0.00	0.00	21,141.00		0.00	25,241.00	0.00	0.00	26,596.00	0.00	0.00
(14,201.00)	0.00	0.00	(1,166.00)		0.00	(11,316.00)	0.00	0.00	6,026.00	0.00	0.00

(28)

OPERATING PLAN FORECAST (P & L Projection)

SBA FORM 1099 (8-85) SOP: 60 10

page 3

Month 6	JUN		Month 7	JUL		Month 8	AUG		Month 9	SEPT	
Estimate	Actual	%	Estimate	Actual	%	Estimate	Actual	%	Estimate	Actual	%
41,496.00			76,608.00			51,072.00			60,750.00		
4,000.00			4,500.00			5,000.00			4,800.00		
2,200.00			2,400.00			2,600.00			2,400.00		
47,696.00	0.00	0.00	83,508.00	0.00	0.00	58,672.00	0.00	0.00	67,950.00	0.00	0.00
20,748.00			38,304.00			25,536.00			30,375.00		
3,000.00			3,250.00			3,500.00			3,400.00		
1,375.00			1,500.00			1,625.00			1,500.00		
25,123.00	0.00	0.00	43,054.00	0.00	0.00	30,661.00	0.00	0.00	35,275.00	0.00	0.00
22,573.00	0.00	0.00	40,454.00	0.00	0.00	28,011.00	0.00	0.00	32,675.00	0.00	0.00
3,520.00			3,520.00			3,520.00			3,520.00		
269.00			269.00			269.00			269.00		
0.00			0.00			0.00			0.00		
18,400.00			18,400.00			20,200.00			20,200.00		
521.00			521.00			521.00			521.00		
30.00			30.00			30.00			30.00		
300.00			300.00			300.00			300.00		
100.00			100.00			100.00			100.00		
400.00			400.00			400.00			400.00		
160.00			160.00			160.00			160.00		
1,300.00			1,300.00			1,300.00			1,300.00		
1,000.00			1,250.00			1,250.00			1,500.00		
290.00			290.00			290.00			290.00		
320.00			320.00			320.00			320.00		
0.00			0.00			0.00			0.00		
1,286.00			1,286.00			1,286.00			1,286.00		
500.00			500.00			500.00			500.00		
28,396.00	0.00	0.00	28,646.00	0.00	0.00	30,446.00	0.00	0.00	30,696.00	0.00	0.00
(5,823.00)	0.00	0.00	11,808.00	0.00	0.00	(2,435.00)	0.00	0.00	1,979.00	0.00	0.00

(29)

OPERATING PLAN FORECAST (P & L Projection)

SBA FORM 1099 (8-85) SOP: 60 10

page 4

Month 10	OCT		Month 11	NOV		Month 12	DEC		1993 TOTAL			
Estimate	Actual	%	Estimate	Actual	%	Estimate	Actual	%	Estimate	%	Actual	%
40,500.00			147,000.00			98,000.00			672,920.00			
4,800.00			5,000.00			5,500.00			46,325.00			
2,400.00			2,200.00			2,200.00			24,680.00			
47,700.00	0.00	0.00	154,200.00	0.00	0.00	105,700.00	0.00	0.00	743,925.00	0.00	0.00	0.00
20,250.00			73,500.00			49,000.00			336,460.00			
3,400.00			3,500.00			3,750.00			35,163.00			
1,500.00			1,375.00			1,375.00			15,425.00			
25,150.00	0.00	0.00	78,375.00	0.00	0.00	54,125.00			387,048.00	0.00	0.00	0.00
22,550.00	0.00	0.00	75,825.00	0.00	0.00	51,575.00	0.00	0.00	356,877.00	0.00	0.00	0.00
3,520.00			3,520.00			3,520.00			38,400.00			
269.00			269.00			269.00			2,920.00			
0.00			0.00			0.00			0.00			
22,000.00			22,000.00			22,000.00			213,600.00			
521.00			521.00			521.00			5,352.00			
30.00			30.00			30.00			360.00			
300.00			300.00			300.00			3,600.00			
100.00			100.00			100.00			1,200.00			
400.00			400.00			400.00			4,800.00			
160.00			160.00			160.00			1,920.00			
1,300.00			1,300.00			1,300.00			15,600.00			
1,500.00			1,800.00			1,800.00			13,700.00			
290.00			290.00			290.00			3,480.00			
320.00			320.00			320.00			3,768.00			
0.00			0.00			0.00			0.00			
1,286.00			1,286.00			1,286.00			15,432.00			
500.00			500.00			500.00			6,000.00			
32,496.00	0.00	0.00	32,796.00	0.00	0.00	32,796.00	0.00	0.00	330,132.00	0.00	0.00	0.00
(9,946.00)	0.00	0.00	43,029.00	0.00	0.00	18,779.00	0.00	0.00	26,745.00	0.00	0.00	0.00

(30)

MARINE ART OF CALIFORNIA

IV. SUPPORTING DOCUMENTS

Personal Resume

Letter of Reference

Proposal for Limited Partnership

Catalog Cost Analysis

Competition Comparison Analysis

Terms and Conditions for Participants

Robert A. Garcia

P.O. Box 10059-251   (714) 722-6478
Newport Beach CA 92658
Manufacturing Management

Record of accomplishments in 12+ years in manufacturing and distribution. Experience in start-up and turnaround operations. In-depth understanding of multi-facility high-tech production systems/methods. Strengths in project management, problem solving and coordinating/managing critical manufacturing functions: purchasing, engineering, inventory control, tracking, scheduling and quality assurance developed with General Dynamics.

PROFILE:

Hands-on management style: coordinated five support groups in Arizona, Arkansas, and California facilities in production of 57 complex assemblies, each having up to 100 components per circuit board.

Experience in product development for target markets; multi-product experience.

Set priorities, provided clear direction, energized others, got positive results.

Enthusiastic rapport builder, analytical self-starter, persistent, persuasive.

ACHIEVEMENT OVERVIEW
Turnaround Operations

Production of systems seven months behind schedule, inventory control unreliable, purchasing not aggressively seeking critical components from vendors.

*   Procured materials for electronic circuit card assemblies in support of off-site and final assembly of missile systems.

*   Created, along with other members of special task team, procedures and internal tracking system to show how specific part shortages would impact production schedules up to six months ahead.

*   Chaired weekly inventory status meetings with Purchasing and Quality Assurance representatives.

*   Supervised five analysts.

*   Coordinated sub-assembly activities between offsite facilities in Arizona and Arkansas and final assembly in California in order to deliver product to customers against tight time constraints.

*   Trained new hires.

*   Provided data analysis to upper management for review.

Corrected inventory accuracy from 70% to 97% within nine months.

(32)

Robert A. Garcia..Page 2

Start-up Production/Distribution - Part Time Operation (secondary income)

* Researched market, found great potential for product, Bonsai trees.

* Studied plant propagation methods, built large greenhouse, implemented methods learned, marketed product.

* Participated in various home and garden shows, county fairs, three major shows/year.

* Employed staff of 8, wholesaled products to nurseries in LA and Orange Counties.

Grew and operated business successfully for eight years, increased net profit from $4500 to $12,000 within four years.

CAREER HISTORY

Freelance Photography/Marine Art of California *Owner/President*	1992 - Current
Sea Fantasies Gallery *Store Manager*	1991 - 1992
General Dynamics Corporation *Manufacturing Coordinator*	1980 - 1989
Casa Vallarta Restaurant *Controller (part -time)*	1986 - 1987
B & D Nursery (secondary income) *Operations Manager*	1973 - 1981
Stater Bros Markets *Journeyman Clerk*	1969 - 1980

EDUCATION

Completed course work in History, California State Polytechnic University. Independent studies in Psychology of Supervision, Written Communication

AFFILIATIONS/INTERESTS

Coordinator on Service Board for Orange County
Alanon and Alateen Family Groups, 1988 - 1990

Regularly cast in musical productions.
Have appeared at Orange County Performing Arts Center and Fullerton Civic Light Opera.

(33)

Powell and Associates
Marketing Consultants

1215 West Imperial Highway - Suite 103 - Brea, CA - 92621 - Keith Powell - President - (714) 680-8306

November 17, 1992

Dear Prospective Investor:

It is indeed a pleasure to write a reference letter for Bob A. Garcia.

I have known Bob over the past five years and have found him to be an extremely creative and enthusiastic individual. I have been associated with Bob through several community and civic organizations for which he is an active participant. He has also held office in several of these organizations and has always fulfilled his duties with aplomb.

Bob approached me well over a year ago to meet with him on a regular basis to become a "mentor" of a then dream, now a reality, his company MARINE ART OF CALIFORNIA. Along with several other mentors that he has been seeking advice from, I have had the privilege of reviewing, commenting and assisting in the development of his plan. He has evidenced great discipline, follow through, creativity and a willingness to do his homework on this business venture.

I would most highly recommend he be given the consideration he seeks. Bob has evidenced the qualities needed to succeed in any business venture, that of commitment, dedication, optimism and follow through.

If you have any further questions, please do not hesitate to contact me. My direct line is 714-680-8306.

Cordially,

Keith P. Powell
President

PROPOSAL FOR LIMITED PARTNERSHIP

Borrow $130,000.00 from private investors as limited partners as outlined:

$130,000.00 = 45% of Marine Art of California
$130,000.00 = 20 shares @ $6,500.00 each
1 share = 2.25% of Marine Art of California

Limited Partners will own 2.25% of the business for each $6,500.00 invested. The investment will be treated as a loan and paid back at 11% interest over 15 years at $78.00 per month.

1 share = $78.00 per month for 6 years
20 shares = $1560.00 per month

The General Partner, Robert A. Garcia, will own 55% of the business. The Limited Partners will own 45% of the business for the duration of the partnership.

The duration of the partnership is 4 years. The General Partner will have the option of buying out the Limited Partners at the end of four years for $3,250.00 for each 2.25% interest. The buyout will not affect the outstanding loan, but the General Partner will provide collateral equal to the loan balance. The value of inventory will be used as that collateral.

Return On Investment (ROI) for each $6,500.00 share:

A. <u>Principal (15 years)</u>   <u>Interest (15 years)</u>   <u>Buy-out (4 years)</u>   <u>Total (15 years)</u>
    $6,500.00   + $6,800.00   + $3,250.00   = $16,500.00

B. PROJECTED Annual Profits (Loss) for 1 share (2.25%):

<u>1992</u>	<u>1993</u>	<u>1994</u>	<u>1995</u>		4 Year Total
($1,090.00)	$590.00	$8,336.00	$14,089.00	=	$21,925.00

Principal & Interest (15 years) $13,300.00
Buy-Out (4 years) $3,250.00
Projected Profits/loss (4 years)   <u>$21,925.00</u>

Total Projected Return on Investment = $38,475.00

Contract Highlights:

1. **1st Right of Refusal:** Limited Partners agree to extend the 1st Right of Refusal to the General Partner, Robert A. Garcia, in the event the Limited Partner desires to sell, grant, or trade his share of the business.

2. **Key Man Insurance:** A Life Insurance Policy valued at $250,000.00 shall be taken out on General Partner, Robert A. Garcia, which is approximately double the amount of the $130,000.00 loan needed. In the event of the death of Robert A Garcia, the payments of the full policy amount will be divided among the Limited Partners equal to the amount invested (eg. 2.25% investment would equal a 1/20th payout of $12,500.00)

3. **Limited Partner Purchase Program:** General Partner, Robert A. Garcia, agrees to grant a **50% discount** on all product line items for the purchase of 3 or more shares. For 1-2 shares, a **40% discount** shall be extended. These shall be in effect for the life of the Limited Partnership Contract (minimum **4 years** before exercising buyout option). For remainder of the loan contract, (2 years) a **discount of 35%** off retail price will be extended. At the completion of the loan repayment, a **Lifetime Discount of 20%** off retail will be extended to Limited Partners. These privileges are non-transferable.

CATALOG COST ANALYSIS

PRINTING QTY	20,000	30,000	40,000	50,000	60,000
CATALOG ITEMS					
24 Page - Price per 1000	521.37	413.92	360.07	336.11	306.49
WEIGHT - 2.208 OZ.					
Extended Cost	10,427.40	12,417.60	14,402.80	16,305.50	18,389.40
Prep & Delivery	756.00	970.00	1,235.00	1,500.00	1,765.00
Mail List Costs - $50 per/1000	1,000.00	1,500.00	2,000.00	2,500.00	3,000.00
Postage - $170 per/1000	3,200.00	4,800.00	6,400.00	8,000.00	9,600.00
Film Separations - $64 per/page	3,600.00	2,500.00	2,500.00	2,500.00	2,500.00
Art Work	1,000.00	1,000.00	1,000.00	1,000.00	1,000.00
TOTAL COSTS	19,983.40	23,187.60	27,537.80	31,805.50	36,254.40
Rounded Numbers	20,000.00	23,200.00	27,600.00	32,000.00	36,500.00
UNIT COSTS	1.00	0.77	0.69	0.64	0.60
COSTS PER PAGE	0.04	0.03	0.03	0.03	0.03
COSTS PER/1000	999.17	772.92	688.44	636.11	604.24

PRINTING QTY	70,000	80,000	90,000	100,000	
CATALOG ITEMS					
24 Page - Price per 1000	291.72	280.29	268.85	261.00	
WEIGHT - 2.208 OZ.					
Extended Cost	20,420.40	22,423.20	24,196.50	26,100.00	
Prep & Delivery	2,030.00	2,295.00	2,560.00	2,825.00	
Mail List Costs - $50 per/1000	3,500.00	4,000.00	4,500.00	5,000.00	
Postage - $170 per/1000	11,900.00	13,600.00	15,300.00	17,000.00	
Film Separations - $64 per/page	2,500.00	2,500.00	2,500.00	2,500.00	
Art Work	1,000.00	1,000.00	1,000.00	1,000.00	
TOTAL COSTS	41,350.40	45,818.20	50,056.50	54,425.00	
Rounded Numbers	41,500.00	46,000.00	50,500.00	55,000.00	
UNIT COSTS	0.59	0.57	0.56	0.54	
COSTS PER PAGE	0.02	0.02	0.02	0.02	
COSTS PER/1000	590.72	572.73	556.18	544.25	
NOTE: 20% will be deducted for	**40,000**	**50,000**	**60,000**	**70,000**	
foreign printing. Prices are	27,600.00	32,000.00	36,500.00	41,500.00	
reflected in Profit Analysis.	0.80	0.80	0.80	0.80	
FOREIGN PRINTING COSTS	22,080.00	25,600.00	29,200.00	33,200.00	
	80,000	**90,000**	**100,000**		
	46,000.00	50,500.00	55,000.00		
	0.80	0.80	0.80		
FOREIGN PRINTING COSTS	36,800.00	40,400.00	44,000.00		

COMPETITION COMPARISON ANALYSIS

	Price Range	Total Retail Prices	Percentage of Total Prices	# of Items	Item RNG %		
COMPANY NAME							
Wild Wings	-50.00	2,092.35	3%	68	19%		
Spring 1992	-100.00	5,269.50	7%	68	19%	-100.00	38%
32 Pages	-200.00	11,302.00	15%	78	22%		
	-500.00	39,905.00	54%	124	35%		
	-999.00	11,045.00	15%	19	5%		
	$1,000.00	4,745.00	6%	2	1%		
		$74,358.85	100%	359	100%		
						Avg Item Price	$207.13
		(Based on keystone pricing)				Avg Item Profit	$103.56
Sharper Image	-50.00	1,580.65	9%	47	39%		
Jul/Aug	-100.00	2,418.45	14%	31	26%	-100.00	64%
24 of 60 Pages	-200.00	3,898.75	23%	25	21%		
	-500.00	4,879.45	29%	13	11%		
	-999.00	2,797.85	17%	4	3%		
	$1,000.00	1,195.00	7%	1	1%		
		$16,770.15	100%	121	100%		
						Avg Item Price	$138.60
		(Based on keystone pricing)				Avg Item Profit	$69.30
Sharper Image	-50.00	2,223.60	10%	73	42%		
Jul/Aug	-100.00	3,227.95	15%	41	24%	-100.00	66%
32 of 60 Pages	-200.00	5,088.35	23%	33	19%		
	-500.00	7,129.10	33%	20	12%		
	-999.00	4,047.75	19%	6	3%		
	$1,000.00	0.00	0%	0	0%		
		$21,716.75	100%	173	100%		
						Avg Item Price	$125.53
		(Based on keystone pricing)				Avg Item Profit	$62.77
Marine Art of California	-50.00	2,826.95	13%	108	54%		
Nov/Dec	-100.00	3,587.65	17%	46	23%	-100.00	77%
40 Pages	-200.00	3,461.85	16%	23	12%		
	-500.00	4,528.25	21%	15	8%		
	-999.00	4,281.00	20%	6	3%		
	$1,000.00	2,600.00	12%	1	1%		
		$21,285.70	100%	199	100%		
						Avg Item Price	$106.96
		(Based on keystone pricing)				Avg Item Profit	$53.48

MARINE ART OF CALIFORNIA
Robert A. Garcia
P.O. Box 10059-251
Newport Beach, CA 92658
(714) 722-6478

TERMS AND CONDITIONS FOR PARTICIPANTS

1. **Artist/Vendor** agrees to have personal or answering system available Monday - Friday, 9:00 AM - 5:00 PM to receive orders. **Marine Art of California** shall be given prior notice (5 working days) if any temporary change in operating hours is to be made.

2. **Artist/Vendor** agrees to drop ship stocked items within 48 hours of notification to indicated customer with Instructions for Shipping provided by **Marine Art of California**. A time schedule is needed for custom made pieces such as bronzes acrylics, or original art works requiring longer delivery. Customer will pay shipping.

3. **Artist/Vendor** agrees to provide 48 hour Federal Express Delivery with added shipping charges for all stocked items.

4. **Artist/Vendor** agrees to use only shipping labels provided by **Marine Art of California**.

5. **Artist/Vendor** guarantees that all items shipped will be free of any business names, logos, addresses, phone numbers or any other printed material referencing said **Artist/Vendor** (engravings or signatures of **Artist** on pieces not included).

6. Each **Artist** shall include a pre-approved autobiographical sheet with each shipment.

7. **Artist/Vendor** shall include required Certificates of Authenticity on all Limited Edition pieces shipped.

8. Exclusive marketing rights for a selected art item made for **Marine Art of California** shall be covered in a separate contract.

9. **Artist/Vendor** agrees to fax a copy of the shipping manifest or phone in shipping information and date of pickup on same day of transaction.

10. **Artist/Vendor** guarantees insurance coverage for the full retail value.

11. **Artist/Vendor** shall agree to 10 day full refund period beginning from the date customer receives shipped merchandise.

12. **Artist/Vendor** agrees to extend 30 days net payment plan to **Marine Art of California**.

13. **Artist/Vendor** shall not record names nor addresses of buyers for purposes of any sales or marketing contact within 24 months of shipment of the order.

Terms and Conditions, page 2

14. In lieu of any participation fee, **Artist/Vendor** agrees to extend a 15% discount on published wholesale prices to **Marine Art of California**. This is justifiable due to advertising, printing, mailing and target marketing costs and project volume sales.

15. Each **Artist/Vendor** shall be notified 2 weeks prior to the mailing of the first catalog issue.

16. **Artist/Vendor** agrees to provide goods and services as stated above for a minimum duration of 60 days after publication date.

I hereby acknowledge and accept these terms and conditions set forth by **Marine Art of California.**

_____
(Company)

_____
(Print Name and Title)

_____
(Signature and Title of Authorized Representative)

Date:_____

(revision date 6/03/92)

APPENDIX **III**

Blank Forms
and Worksheets

Ready to Copy for Your Own Use

The forms on the following pages have been provided for you to copy and use in the writing of your business plan.

The forms that contain "Variable Expenses" and "Fixed Expenses" have spaces for you to fill in your own categories. They should be customized to your particular business. This will require you to decide on category headings when you begin the financial section of your business plan and follow through with the same headings throughout all financial statements.

The categories are developed by looking at your different accounts in your ledger or by using the categories from your revenue and expense journal. Those expenses that are frequent and sizable will have a heading of their own (ex: advertising, rent, salaries, etc.). Those expenses that are very small and infrequent will be included under the heading "miscellaneous" in either the variable or fixed expenses section of each of your financial statements.

CASH TO BE PAID OUT WORKSHEET
(CASH FLOWING OUT OF THE BUSINESS)

1. START-UP COSTS
   a. Business License $ _____
   b. Corporation Filing   _____
   c. Legal Fees   _____
   d. Other start-up costs:

   _____   _____
   _____   _____
   _____   _____

2. INVENTORY PURCHASES
   Cash out for goods intended for resale   _____

3. VARIABLE EXPENSES (SELLING/DIRECT)
   a. $ _____
   b.   _____
   c.   _____
   d.   _____
   e.   _____
   f.   _____
   g. Miscell. Selling Expense   _____
   TOTAL SELLING EXPENSES   _____

4. FIXED EXPENSES (ADMINISTRATIVE/INDIRECT)
   a. $ _____
   b.   _____
   c.   _____
   d.   _____
   e.   _____
   f.   _____
   g. Miscell. Admin. Expense   _____
   TOTAL OPERATING EXPENSE   _____

5. ASSETS (LONG-TERM PURCHASES)
   Cash to be paid out in current period   _____

6. LIABILITIES
   Cash outlay for retiring debts, loans
   and/or accounts payable   _____

7. OWNER EQUITY
   Cash to be withdrawn by owner   _____

TOTAL CASH TO BE PAID OUT $ _____

SOURCES OF CASH WORKSHEET

(CASH FLOWING INTO THE BUSINESS)

1. CASH ON HAND $ _____

2. SALES (REVENUES)

Sales Income _____

Services Income _____

Deposits on Sales or Services _____

Collections on Accounts Receivable _____

3. MISCELLANEOUS INCOME

Interest Income _____

Payments to be Received on Loans _____

4. SALE OF LONG-TERM ASSETS _____

5. LIABILITIES _____

Loan Funds (To be received during period
from banks, SBA and other lending institutions)

6. EQUITY

Owner Investments (Sole Prop/Partners) _____

Contributed Capital (Corporation) _____

Sale of Stock (Corporation) _____

Venture Capital _____

TOTAL CASH AVAILABLE: **A.** *Without Sales* $ _____

B. *With Sales* $ _____

PRO FORMA CASH FLOW STATEMENT

Company Name: _____

FOR THE YEAR 19___	TOTAL	JAN	FEB	MAR	APR	MAY	JUN	JUL	AUG	SEP	OCT	NOV	DEC
BEGINNING CASH BALANCE													
CASH RECEIPTS													
a. Sales revenues (Cash sales)													
b. Receivables to be collected													
c. Interest income													
d. Sale of long-term assets													
TOTAL CASH AVAILABLE													
CASH PAYMENTS													
a. Cost of goods to be sold													
1. Purchases													
2. Material													
3. Labor													
b. Variable expenses (Selling, Direct)													
1.													
2.													
3.													
4.													
5.													
6.													
7. Miscellaneous Variable Expenses													
c. Fixed expenses (Administrative, Indirect)													
1.													
2.													
3.													
4.													
5.													
6.													
7. Miscellaneous Fixed Expenses													
d. Interest expense													
e. Federal income tax													
f. Other uses													
g. Payments on long-term assets													
h. Loan Payment													
i. Owner draws													
TOTAL CASH PAID OUT													
CASH BALANCE/DEFICIENCY													
LOANS TO BE RECEIVED													
EQUITY DEPOSITS													
ENDING CASH BALANCE													

QUARTERLY BUDGET ANALYSIS

Company Name: _____

For the Quarter Ending _____, 19 ____   YTD = year-to-date

BUDGET ITEM	BUDGET THIS QUARTER	ACTUAL THIS QUARTER	VARIATION THIS QUARTER	YTD BUDGET	ACTUAL YTD	VARIATION YTD
SALES REVENUES						
Less Cost of Goods						
GROSS PROFIT						
VARIABLE EXPENSES						
1.						
2.						
3.						
4.						
5.						
6.						
7. Miscellaneous						
FIXED EXPENSES						
1.						
2.						
3.						
4.						
5.						
6.						
7. Miscellaneous						
NET INCOME FROM OPERATIONS						
INTEREST INCOME						
INTEREST EXPENSE						
NET PROFIT (LOSS) BEFORE TAXES						
TAXES						
NET PROFIT (LOSS) AFTER TAXES						
NON-INCOME STATEMENT ITEMS						
1. L-Term Asset Repay'ts						
2. Loan Repayments						
3. Owner Draws						

BUDGET DEVIATIONS	Current Quarter	Year-To-Date
1. Income Statement Items:	$	$
2. Non-Income Statement Items:	$	$
3. Total Deviation (1+2)	$	$

THREE-YEAR
INCOME PROJECTION

FOR THE YEARS 19___, 19___ AND 19___.	YEAR 1	YEAR 2	YEAR 3
INCOME			
1. NET SALES. (Gross less returns & allow.)			
2. COST OF GOODS SOLD (c. minus d.)			
a. Beginning Inventory			
b. Purchases			
c. C.O.G. Available for Sale (a+b)			
d. Less End. Inv. (Dec. 31st)			
3. GROSS PROFIT ON SALES (1 minus 2)			
EXPENSES			
1. VARIABLE (Direct/Selling) (a. thru h.)			
a.			
b.			
c.			
d.			
e.			
f.			
g. Miscellaneous Selling Exp.			
h. Depreciation (Product/Services Assets)			
2. FIXED (Indirect/Administrative) (a. thru h.)			
a.			
b.			
c.			
d.			
e.			
f.			
g. Miscell. Administrative Expense			
h. Depreciation (Office Equipment)			
TOTAL OPERATING EXPENSES (Variable+Fixed)			
NET INCOME FROM OPERATIONS (Gross Profit less Expenses)			
OTHER INCOME (INTEREST)			
OTHER EXPENSE (INTEREST)			
NET PROFIT (LOSS) BEFORE INCOME TAXES			
TAXES (Federal, Self-Employment, State)			
NET PROFIT (LOSS) AFTER TAXES			

BREAK-EVEN ANALYSIS

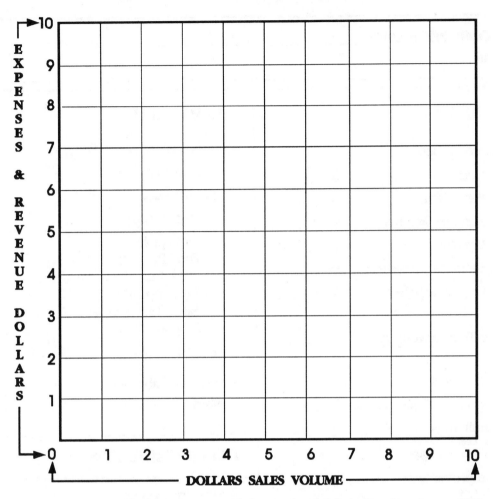

Note: Figures shown in _____ of thousands of dollars (Ex: 2 = $____,000)

B-E Point (Sales) = Fixed Costs + $\left[\dfrac{\text{Variable Costs}}{\text{Estimated Revenues}} \times \text{Sales}\right]$

B-E Point (Sales) = $\$ \qquad + \left[\dfrac{\$}{\$}\underline{\qquad} \times S\right]$

B-E Point (Sales) = $\$ \qquad + \left[\quad \times S\right]$

$S = \$ \qquad + \qquad S$

$S - \qquad S = \$ \qquad$

$\qquad S = \$ \qquad$

$S = \dfrac{\$\underline{\qquad}}{\underline{\qquad}}$

Break-Even Point

$S = \$ \boxed{}$

BALANCE SHEET

COMPANY NAME: _____

Date: _____ ___, 19___

ASSETS

Current Assets

Cash $ _____

Petty Cash $ _____

Accounts Receivable $ _____

Inventory $ _____

Short-Term Investments $ _____

Prepaid Expenses $ _____

Long-Term Investments $ _____

Fixed Assets

Land   (valued at cost) $ _____

Buildings $ _____
1. Cost   _____
2. Less Acc. Depr.   _____

Improvements $ _____
1. Cost   _____
2. Less Acc. Depr.   _____

Equipment $ _____
1. Cost   _____
2. Less Acc. Depr.   _____

Furniture $ _____
1. Cost   _____
2. Less Acc. Depr.   _____

Autos/Vehicles $ _____
1. Cost   _____
2. Less Acc. Depr.   _____

Other Assets
1. $ _____
2. $ _____

TOTAL ASSETS $ _____

LIABILITIES

Current Liabilities

Accounts Payable $ _____

Notes Payable $ _____

Interest Payable $ _____

Taxes Payable
Fed. Inc. Tax $ _____
State Inc. Tax $ _____
Self-Emp. Tax $ _____
Sales Tax Accrual $ _____
Property Tax $ _____

Payroll Accrual $ _____

Long-Term Liabilities
Notes Payable $ _____

TOTAL LIABILITIES $ _____

NET WORTH

Proprietorship $ _____
or
Partnership

(Name's) Equity $ _____
(Name's) Equity $ _____
or
Corporation

Capital Stock $ _____
Surplus Paid In $ _____
Retained Earnings $ _____

TOTAL NET WORTH $ _____

Assets - Liabilities = Net Worth

Total Liabilities and Equity will
always be equal to Total Assets

PROFIT & LOSS STATEMENT (INCOME STATEMENT)

Company Name: _____

FOR THE YEAR 19___	JAN	FEB	MAR	APR	MAY	JUN	JUL	AUG	SEP	OCT	NOV	DEC	YEAR TOTAL
INCOME													
1. NET SALES (Gross less ret. & allow.)													
2. COST OF GOODS SOLD (c. - d.)													
a. Beginning Inventory													
b. Purchases													
c. C.O.G. Available for Sale (a+b)													
d. Less End. Inv. (Dec. 31st)													
3. GROSS PROFIT ON SALES (1. minus 2.)													
EXPENSES													
1. VARIABLE (Selling/Direct Exp.) (a. thru h.)													
a.													
b.													
c.													
d.													
e.													
f.													
g.													
h. Miscell. Selling Exp.													
2. FIXED (Administrative/Indirect) (a. thru h.)													
a.													
b.													
c.													
d.													
e.													
f.													
g.													
h. Miscell. Overhead													
TOTAL OPERATING EXPENSE (Variable+Fixed)													
NET INCOME FROM OPERATIONS (Gross Profit less Operating Expense)													
OTHER INCOME (INTEREST)													
OTHER EXPENSE (INTEREST)													
NET PROFIT (LOSS) BEFORE INCOME TAXES													
TAXES (Federal, Self-Employment, State)													
NET PROFIT (LOSS) AFTER TAXES													

PROFIT & LOSS (INCOME) STATEMENT

COMPANY NAME: _____

For the period beginning _____ and ending _____

INCOME		
1. **NET SALES** (Gross less ret. & allow.)		
2. **COST OF GOODS SOLD** (c. minus d.)		
a. Beginning Inventory		
b. Purchases		
c. C.O.G. Available for Sale (a+b)		
d. Less End. Inv. (Dec. 31st)		
3. **GROSS PROFIT ON SALES** (1 minus 2)		
EXPENSES		
1. **VARIABLE (Selling/Direct)** (a. thru h.)		
a.		
b.		
c.		
d.		
e.		
f.		
g.		
h. Miscellaneous		
2. **FIXED (Administrative/Indirect)** (a. thru h.)		
a.		
b.		
c.		
d.		
e.		
f.		
g.		
h. Miscellaneous		
TOTAL OPERATING EXPENSE (1 + 2)		
NET INCOME FROM OPERATIONS (Gross Profit less Total Op.Exp.)		
OTHER INCOME (INTEREST)		
OTHER EXPENSE (INTEREST)		
NET PROFIT (LOSS) BEFORE INCOME TAXES		
TAXES (Federal, Self-Employment, State)		
NET PROFIT (LOSS) AFTER TAXES		

Index

V

variable expense budget, 46

W

Worst-Best Case Scenarios, 20, 30, 35